ALPHABET THEME-A-SAURUS®

The Great Big Book of Alphabet Teaching Themes

Compiled by **Jean Warren**

Illustrated by **Gary Mohrmann**

Totline® Books

Warren Publishing House
Everett, Washington

D1400728

Special thanks to Jeannie Lybecker, children's literature specialist, for compiling a list of children's books for each unit.

Editorial Staff: Gayle Bittinger, Elizabeth McKinnon, Susan M. Sexton, Jean Warren
Contributing Editor: Susan M. Paprocki
Production Coordinator: Eileen Carbary
Design: Kathy Jones
Computer Graphics: Eric Stovall, André Samson, David Herman

ISBN 0-911019-38-3

Library of Congress Catalog Number 90-071272
Printed in the United States of America
Published by: Warren Publishing House
                P.O. Box 2250
                Everett, WA 98203

20 19 18 17 16 15 14 13 12 11 10 9 8 7

CONTENTS

INTRODUCTION

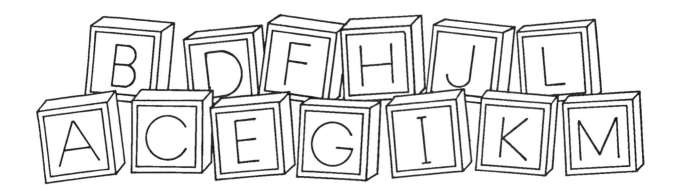

   Alphabet Theme-A-Saurus is designed as a resource for introducing young children to the ABC's. The book is filled with easy hands-on activities that invite children to sing, move and experience alphabet letters in creative and playful ways. Even very young children can participate in the activities and feel comfortable with their letter recognition abilities.

   In *Alphabet Theme-A-Saurus* you will find a unit for each letter of the alphabet plus an Alphabet Review unit that provides ideas for working with more than one letter. Each letter unit contains a collection of activities from a variety of curriculum areas such as art, language, learning games, science, music, movement and snacks. Although the activities are based on letter recognition, through association many children will begin to group words that have similar beginning sounds. If you work with older children, you can easily incorporate the teaching of beginning sounds as part of the activities.

At the end of each letter unit are two special features: puppet patterns to accompany an animal song and an occupation song, plus a set of alphabet card patterns. The patterns may be photocopied to create letter recognition games. The patterns may also be used to make individual books for the children.

As you work with the units in this book, you will find that opportunities for teaching letter recognition skills are everywhere. Feel free to take advantage of these opportunities, incorporating your own ideas and encouraging your children to explore their world for signs of new letters. With *Alphabet Theme-A-Saurus* as a resource, you can help make their learning of the ABC's an adventure of fun and discovery.

Jean Warren

The Letter A

Display/Play Box for A

Decorate a box with the letter A to use throughout your A unit. Inside the box place items (or pictures of items) whose names begin with A. Below are some suggestions.

- ace
- acorn
- acrobat
- airplane
- album
- alligator
- anchor
- angel
- ant
- apple
- apron
- arrow
- astronaut
- avocado
- ox

Apple A's

Cut large letter A shapes out of heavy paper. Set out glue and pictures of apples cut from magazines and seed catalogs. Let the children glue the apple pictures on their A shapes. If desired, let them also attach a few apple stickers.

Variation: Cut small apples in half and pat the cut surfaces dry with paper towels. Let the children dip the apple halves into red paint and press them on their A shapes to make apple prints.

My A Book

Make a book for each child by stapling several pieces of white paper together with a construction paper cover. Print "My A Book" and the child's name on the front. Set out magazine pictures of things whose names begin with A, along with upper- and lower-case A's cut from ads or article titles. Let the children choose the pictures and letters they want and glue them on their book pages. Later, arrange a time for the children to "read" their books to you.

Variation: Make books by cutting red construction paper covers and white pages into apple shapes.

A, A, What Can I Say?

A, A, what can I say?
Just what can I say about the letter A?

Airplane and alligator start with an A.
Acorn and apple begin the same way.

Anchor and astronaut start with A too,
As do apron and acrobat, to name just a few.

Abracadabra begins with an A.
It's a magical word that I like to say.

Ant and ax both start with A.
Let's hear it for A! Hip, hip, hurray!

Susan M. Paprocki

The Letter A

A's on the Airplane

Cut a large airplane shape out of butcher paper and label it with the letter A. Place the shape on the floor, along with items from your A Display/Play Box (see page 6). Explain to the children that the airplane has to be loaded with A items before it can take off. Let the children take turns choosing an item, naming it and placing it on the airplane shape. When the airplane is fully loaded, name all the A items with the group.

A Tree

Make a tree out of felt and place it on a flannelboard. Put a felt letter A on the tree trunk. Cut apple shapes from construction paper and glue on pictures of things whose names begin with A. Attach felt strips to the backs of the apple shapes and place the apples on the tree. Let the children take turns picking apples from the tree and naming the things that are pictured on them.

Apron A's

Label the pocket of an apron with the letter A and put on the apron. Cut index cards in half. Print A's on most of the cards and print other letters on the rest. Spread out the cards on a table. Then let the children take turns selecting A cards from the table and putting them into your apron pocket.

Variation: Use an apron that has two pockets. Have the children place upper-case A cards in one pocket and lower-case A cards in the other.

A Is for Aces

Put together a deck of playing cards that includes the aces from several decks. Let the children sort through the cards to find the aces. If desired, have them place the red aces in one pile and the black aces in another.

Sorting Triangles

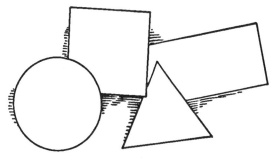

Point out to the children that the upper-case A is shaped like a triangle. Set out a box containing posterboard circles, squares, triangles and rectangles. Let the children take turns sorting through the shapes to find the triangles.

The Letter A

Acrobatic A's

Divide the children into groups of threes. Have the children in each group lie on the floor and use their bodies to form the letter A. Let the children in each group trade places and form the letter A again. Then have the children gather in larger groups and have fun forming giant A's.

Let's Sing Hurray for A
Sung to: "The Farmer in the Dell"

Let's sing hurray for A,
Let's sing hurray for A.
Let's sing hurray for A today,
Let's sing hurray for A!

Apple and *ant* start with A,
Asparagus starts the same way.
Let's sing hurray for A today,
Let's sing hurray for A!

Repeat, substituting other words that begin with A for the words "apple," "ant" and "asparagus."

Elizabeth McKinnon

More Ideas for Fun With A

- Do aerobic exercises.
- Make fingerprint ants on an ant hill shape.
- Act out animal movements.
- Trace A's with fingers on one another's arms.
- Pretend to be airplanes flying through the air.
- Form A's with segments of drinking straws.
- Glue pictures of A items on a giant A shape.
- Start an avocado plant from seed.
- Fill an album with pictures of A items.

Applesauce

Let the children help make applesauce for snacktime. Quarter, core and peel 3 to 4 sweet apples. Cut the quarter pieces in half and place them in a saucepan. Add $\frac{1}{2}$ cup water, sprinkle on $\frac{1}{2}$ teaspoon cinnamon and simmer, covered, until the apples are tender. Let the children mash the cooked apples with a potato masher. Then spoon the cooled applesauce into small bowls. Makes 6 servings.

Children's Books:

- *Alistair in Outer Space*, Marilyn Sadler, (Prentice Hall).
- *Aminal*, Lorna Balian, (Abingdon).
- *Arthur's Teacher Trouble*, Mark Brown, (Little Brown).
- *Bill and Pete*, Tomie De Paola, (Putnam).
- *Space Case*, Edward Marshall, (Dial).
- *There's an Alligator Under My Bed*, Mercer Mayer, (Dial).

The Letter A

Did You Ever See an Alligator?
Sung to: "Did You Ever See a Lassie?"

Did you ever see an alligator,
An alligator, an alligator,
Did you ever see an alligator
With great big sharp teeth?
He lies still all day
And winks at his prey.
Did you ever see an alligator
With great big sharp teeth?

Did you ever see an alligator,
An alligator, an alligator,
Did you ever see an alligator
With great big sharp teeth?
He's fat and he's green
And, oh, so mean.
Did you ever see an alligator
With great big sharp teeth?

Jean Warren

Astronaut Song
Sung to: "If You're Happy and You
   Know It"

Outer space is where I really like to go,
I ride inside a space ship, don't you know?
I like to travel through the stars,
Wave to Jupiter and Mars.
Outer space is where I really like to go.

Kristine Wagoner

Contributors:
Betty Ruth Baker, Waco, TX
Jan Bodenstedt, Jackson, MI
Kristine Wagoner, Puyallup, WA

Alphabet Patterns
Use the patterns on the following
pages to make stick puppets, learning games, alphabet books and
other teaching aids.

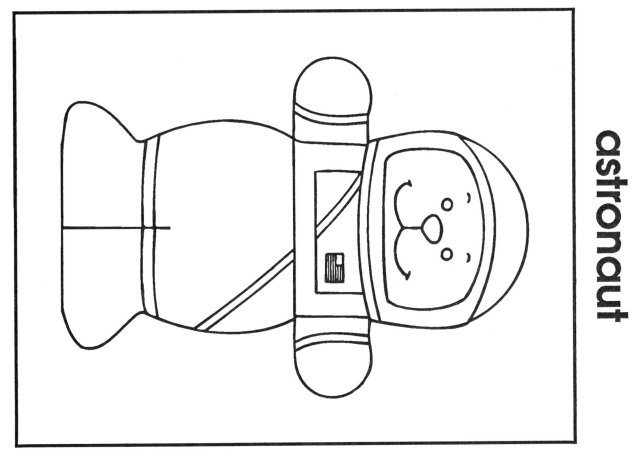

alligator

astronaut

The Letter A　　**13**

Aa

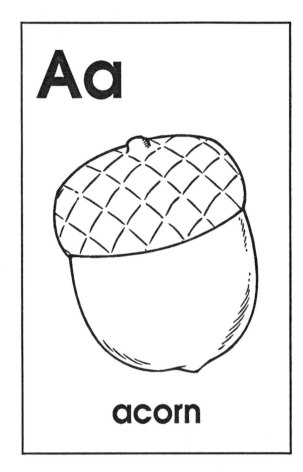

acorn

Aa

airplane

Aa

alligator

Aa

anchor

Aa

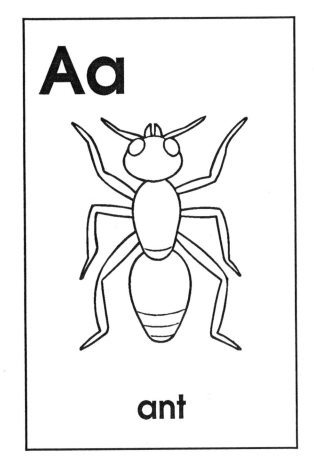

ant

Aa

apple

Aa

apron

Aa

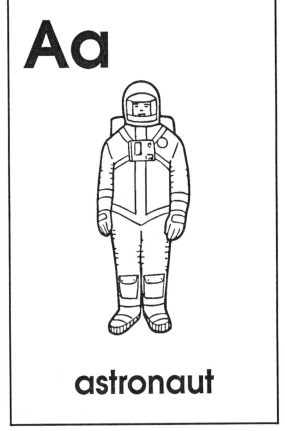

astronaut

The Letter B

Display/Play Box for *B*

Decorate a box with the letter *B* to use throughout your *B* unit. Inside the box place items (or pictures of items) whose names begin with *B*. Below are some suggestions.

- ball
- balloon
- banana
- bandage
- basket
- bat
- bear
- bed
- bell
- belt
- bib
- blanket
- block
- boat
- bone
- book
- boot
- bottle
- bow
- bowl
- bracelet
- brush
- bucket
- butterfly

Button *B*'s

Cut large letter *B* shapes out of heavy paper. Set out glue and a box of buttons. Let the children choose the buttons they want and glue them all over their letter shapes.

Variation: Have the children glue bows or dried beans on their *B* shapes.

Blue Bubble Prints

In a small margarine tub mix one part blue liquid tempera paint with two parts liquid dishwashing detergent and stir in a small amount of water. Let one child at a time put a straw into the paint mixture and blow through it until the bubbles rise above the rim of the margarine tub. Then lay a piece of paper on top of the bubbles and let the child rub across it gently. As the bubbles break, they will leave delicate blue prints on the paper. When the children have finished, print the letter *B* on their papers.

Hint: To help prevent the children from accidentally sucking up the paint mixture, poke holes near the tops of the straws.

Bowing for *B*

Print the letter *B* on five or six index cards and print other letters on several more cards. Ask the children to stand in front of you. Hold up the cards, one at a time, and have the children bow each time they see the letter *B*.

Variation: Hand out bells to the children. Each time they see the letter *B*, have them ring their bells.

B, B, What Begins With *B*?

Place your *B* Display/Play Box (see page 16) on the floor. Take out the items inside and arrange them in front of the box. Have the children sit with you in a semicircle. Start the game by saying, "*B, B*, What begins with *B*? Take a look and you will see what begins with the letter *B*." Then choose a child to pick up one of the items, name it and place it in the box. Continue until each child has had a turn.

The Letter B

B Birds in the Birdhouse

Make a "birdhouse" by turning a large box upside down and cutting a hole in one side. Mark the birdhouse with the letter B. Cut bird shapes out of construction paper. Print the letter B on most of the shapes and print other letters on the rest. Explain to the children that only the B birds can go into the birdhouse. Then let them take turns choosing a bird shape and deciding whether to place it inside the birdhouse or leave it out. Continue until all the B birds are in the birdhouse.

Pat-A-Cake

Play Pat-A-Cake with the children while reciting the following rhyme:

Pat-a-cake, pat-a-cake, baker's man,
Bake me a cake as fast as you can.
Roll it and pat it and mark it with B,
And put it in the oven for Baby and me.

Traditional

Extension: Let the children roll and pat playdough into "cakes." Then let them mark their cakes with a B-shaped cookie cutter.

Balloon *B*'s

Select a balloon for each child. Partially blow up each balloon, print the letter *B* on it with a permanent felt-tip marker and then deflate it. Have the children sit with you in a circle. Blow up the balloons and have the children watch as the *B*'s grow bigger and bigger. Then tie the balloons with string to the children's wrists.

Six Buzzing Bumblebees

Cut six ovals out of black felt. Glue yellow felt strips on the ovals to make simple felt bees. If desired, label each bee with a sticker *B* or a felt *B*. Place the bees on a flannelboard. As you recite the poem below, remove the bees one at a time.

Six buzzing bumblebees
Flying around the hive,
One buzzes off
And that leaves five.

Five buzzing bumblebees
Flying near my door,
One buzzes off
And that leaves four.

Four buzzing bumblebees
Flying around a tree,
One buzzes off
And that leaves three.

Three buzzing bumblebees
In the sky so blue,
One buzzes off
And that leaves two.

Two buzzing bumblebees
Flying by the sun
One buzzes off
And that leaves one.

One buzzing bumblebee
Looking for some fun,
It buzzes off
And that leaves none.

Susan M. Paprocki

The Letter B

Beanbag Boogie

Have the children stand in a circle and give them each a beanbag. Each time you sing the song below, have the children hold or balance their beanbags in a different way (in their hands, on their heads, on their shoulders, on their feet, etc.).

Sung to: "Hokey-Pokey"

You put your beanbag in,
You put your beanbag out,
You put your beanbag in
And you shake it all about.
You do the Beanbag Boogie
And you have a lot of fun.
That's what it's all about.

Rita Galloway

Extension: Put on some music and let the children play Follow the Leader, holding or balancing their beanbags as the leader does. Continue until each child has had a turn leading the line.

More Ideas for Fun With *B*

- Bounce balls.
- Make bead bracelets.
- Bat balloons into the air.
- Trace *B*'s with fingers on one another's backs while making buzzing sounds.
- Walk a balance beam.
- Form a *B* on the floor with beanbags and walk around the letter as it is written.
- Have a Blue Day, a Black Day or a Brown Day.
- Brush teddy bears with a clothes brush.
- Go barefoot.

B, B, B

Sung to: "Three Blind Mice"

B, B, B; B, B, B,
How many B's can I see?
There's B for butterflies in the air,
B for buttons found here and there,
B for bears found everywhere
B, B, B.

Repeat, substituting other words that begin with B for the words "butterflies," "buttons" and "bears."

Jean Warren

B Banquet

If desired, cover the snack table with a blue tablecloth. Set out such foods as bread or biscuits, butter, banana slices and blueberries. Then let the children sit down and enjoy having a "B banquet."

Variation: Let the children help make banana bread (see page 169) to eat as part of their banquet.

Children's Books:
- *Ask Mr. Bear*, Marjorie Flack, (Macmillan).
- *Benjamin's Barn*, Reeve Lindbergh, (Dial).
- *Building a House*, Byron Barton, (Penguin).
- *Peace at Last*, Jill Murphy, (Dial).
- *This Is the Bread I Baked for Ned*, Crescent Dragonwagon, (Macmillan).
- *Toolbox*, Anne Rockwell, (Macmillan).

The Letter B

Little Bear
Sung to: "Three Blind Mice"

Little bear, little bear,
Has brown hair, has brown hair.
He likes to run around and play,
Chasing bumblebees all day,
He likes to roll in the grass this way.
Little bear.

Little bear, little bear,
Has white hair, has white hair.
She likes to swim around and play,
Chasing seals and fish all day,
She likes to roll in the snow this way.
Little bear.

Jean Warren

I'm a Builder
Sung to: "Frere Jacques"

I'm a builder, I'm a builder,
Build, build, build; build, build, build.
Building homes is what I do,
Watch me while I build a few.
Build, build, build; build, build, build.

Here's my hammer, here's my hammer,
Pound, pound, pound;
Pound, pound, pound.
Pounding nails is what I do,
Watch me while I pound a few.
Pound, pound, pound;
Pound, pound, pound.

Here's my saw, here's my saw,
Saw, saw, saw; saw, saw, saw.
Sawing boards is what I do,
Watch me while I saw a few.
Saw, saw, saw; saw, saw, saw.

Elizabeth McKinnon

Contributors:
Betty Ruth Baker, Waco, TX
Jan Bodenstedt, Jackson, MI
Rita Galloway, Harlingen, TX
Judith E. McNitt, Adrian, MI

Alphabet Patterns
Use the patterns on the following pages to make stick puppets, learning games, alphabet books and other teaching aids.

bear

builder

The Letter *B*   23

Bb

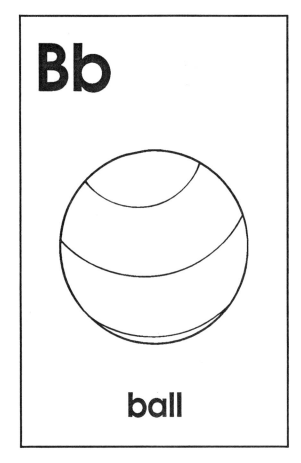

ball

Bb

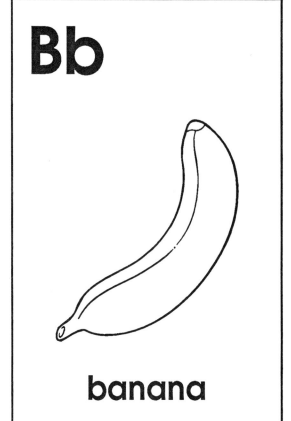

banana

Bb

basket

Bb

bear

Bb

bed

Bb

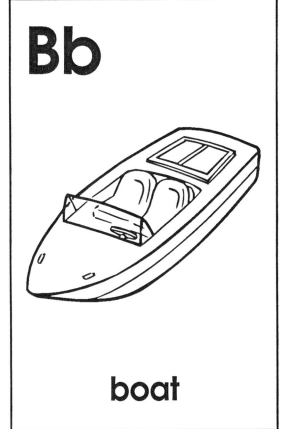

boat

Bb

book

Bb

butterfly

The Letter C

Display/Play Box for *C*

Decorate a box with the letter *C* to use throughout your *C* unit. Inside the box place items (or pictures of items) whose names begin with *C*. Below are some suggestions.

- cake
- camera
- can
- candle
- canoe
- car
- card
- carpet square
- carrot
- chalk
- clock
- clothespin
- clown
- coat
- comb
- cookies
- corn
- cotton
- cowboy hat
- crayon
- crown

Cotton Ball *C*'s

Cut large letter *C* shapes out of heavy paper. Set out cotton balls and shallow containers of glue. Let the children dip the cotton balls into the glue and then place them all over their letter shapes.

Variation: Instead of cotton balls, have the children glue on corn kernels, cornmeal or dried coffee grounds.

Cat Collages

Have the children look through magazines and tear or cut out pictures of cats. (Let younger children choose from precut pictures placed in a box.) Give each child a sheet of construction paper with the letter C printed on it. Let the children glue their pictures on their papers any way they wish to create cat collages.

Variation: Let the children make collages with pictures of cars.

Cutting Corners

Provide the children with squares, rectangles and triangles cut from such materials as construction paper, wallpaper, greeting cards and giftwrap. Let the children use scissors to cut off all the corners. If desired, have them glue their shapes and corners (or just their corners) on sheets of construction paper.

The Letter C

Carpet Square Game

Mark a carpet square with the letter C and place it on the floor. Have the children form a circle, with one child standing on the carpet square. Place your C Display/Play Box (see page 26) in the middle of the circle. Then play music and have the children march around, crossing over the carpet square as they do so. When you stop the music, have the child standing on the carpet square reach into the box, take out an item and name it. Continue the game until everyone has had a turn.

Cabbie Game

Make "tickets" by cutting index cards in half. Print the letter C on most of the cards and print other letters on the rest. Spread out the tickets on a table. Make "cabs" by putting two chairs together, one behind the other. Let half of the children pretend to be cabbies and sit in the front chairs. Let the rest of the children pretend to be passengers. Explain that to take a cab ride, the passengers must each find a C ticket on the table and show it to a cabbie before sitting down in the back seat of the cab. Let the passengers move from cab to cab and ride

to different imaginary destinations. Then have the cabbies and the passengers trade places.

C Clothes on the Clothesline

Cut clothes shapes out of construction paper. Print the letter C on most of the shapes and print other letters on the rest. Hang a clothesline between two chairs and set out a basket of clothespins. Let the children take turns sorting through the clothes shapes and clipping those that are marked with C to the clothesline.

Sorting C's

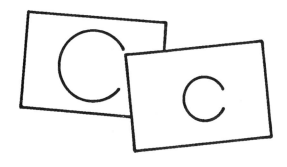

Print upper- and lower-case C's on separate index cards. Be sure to make the lower-case C's noticeably smaller than the upper-case C's. Mix up the cards and let the children take turns sorting them into two piles.

Counting Cans

Set out fifteen empty cans (make sure that any rough edges have been smoothed over). Label five cardboard cartons from 1 to 5. Let the children take turns counting out the cans while placing the appropriate number in each carton.

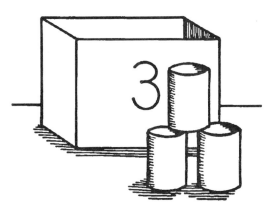

The Letter C

Candid Camera

Play music and let the children dance around the room. When you stop the music, have the children freeze in place. Then use an old camera to snap a pretend picture of the group. Continue playing the game, letting the children take turns holding the camera and taking pictures.

More Ideas for Fun With *C*

- Clap to music.
- Crawl like caterpillars or crabs.
- Curl fingers into *C*'s to make "claws."
- Conduct music while listening to instrumental recordings.
- Trace over sandpaper *C*'s with chalk or cinnamon sticks.
- Climb stairs or pretend mountains.
- Count cookie shapes that have been placed in a cookie jar.

C Song
Sung to: "Skip to my Lou"

Carrots, castles, candy canes,
Cucumbers and clouds with rain,
Cats and cookies, crayons too.
I think C is cool. Don't you?

Cathi Ulbright

C Snacks

At snacktime let the children enjoy such foods as crackers and cheese, cucumber slices or carrot and celery sticks. Talk about the crispy crunchy textures of the crackers and vegetables. Serve with cups of cranberry juice, if desired.

Variation: Use a favorite recipe to make cornbread. Or do any kind of cup cooking.

Children's Books:
- *Cat and Canary*, Michael Foreman, (Dial).
- *Chicka Chicka Boom Boom*, Bill Martin, (Simon & Schuster).
- *Crocodile Beat*, Gail Jorgensen, (Bradbury).
- *Cross Country Cat*, Mary Calhoun, (Morrow).
- *Strega Nona*, Tomie De Paola, (Prentice Hall).
- *Wombat Stew*, Marcia Vaughan, (Silver Burdett).

The Letter C

I'm a Little Cat
Sung to: "I'm a Little Teapot"

I'm a little cat,
Soft and furry.
I'll be your friend,
So don't you worry.
Right up on your lap I like to hop,
I'll purr, purr, purr and never stop.

Betty Silkunas

I'm a Cook
Sung to: "Three Blind Mice"

I'm a cook, I'm a cook,
See me look in my book.
First I'll decide what I should make,
Perhaps some cookies I will bake,
Or if it's your birthday,
I'll bake you a cake.
I'm a cook.

Jean Warren

Contributors:

Jan Bodenstedt, Jackson, MI
Betty Silkunas, Lansdale, PA
Cathi Ulbright, Wooster, OH

Alphabet Patterns

Use the patterns on the following pages to make stick puppets, learning games, alphabet books and other teaching aids.

cat

cook

The Letter C   **33**

Cc

camera

Cc

candle

Cc

car

Cc

carrot

Cc

clock

Cc

clown

Cc

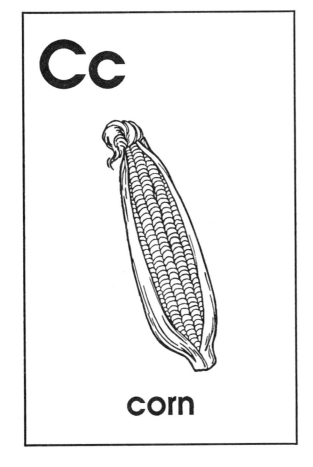

corn

Cc

cow

The Letter D

Display/Play Box for *D*

Decorate a box with the letter *D* to use throughout your *D* unit. Inside the box place items (or pictures of items) whose names begin with *D*. Below are some suggestions.

- daisy
- dandelion
- deer
- diaper
- dice
- dime
- dinosaur
- dishpan
- dog

- doll
- domino
- donkey
- door
- doughnut
- dress
- drum
- duck
- dustpan

Dot *D*'s

Cut large letter *D* shapes out of heavy paper. Let the children decorate their letters by attaching different colored self-stick dots.

Variation: Use a hole punch to punch small circles out of construction paper. Have the children glue the circle "dots" on their *D* shapes.

Dancing Dinosaurs

For each child cut two dinosaur shapes out of brown paper bags or brown butcher paper. Have the children hold their shapes together while you staple around three sides. Then let them crumple small pieces of newspaper and stuff them into their dinosaur shapes. When the shapes are full, staple the remaining sides closed. Let the children deco- rate their stuffed dinosaurs with paint. When the dinosaurs are dry, attach loops of yarn to them for handles. Give each child a sticker with the letter *D* printed on it to attach to his or her dinosaur. Then let the children hold their dinosaurs

D's in the Drawer

Print the letter *D* on an index card and attach the card to an empty drawer. Place the drawer on the floor, along with your *D* Display/Play Box (see page 36). Have the children sit with you in a circle. Let one child begin by taking an item from the box, naming it and then placing the item in the drawer. Continue until each child has had at least one turn.

Extension: At the end of the game ask the children to find a dime in the drawer, a dinosaur in the drawer, etc.

The Letter D

Daisy Flannelboard Game

Cut a large yellow daisy center and white daisy petals out of felt. Print the letter D on the daisy center with a felt-tip marker and place the daisy center on a flannelboard. Print D's and other letters on the daisy petals. Mix up the petals and arrange them on the flannelboard around the daisy center. Then let the children take turns picking off the petals that are not marked with D's.

Drumming for *D*

Print the letter D on five or six index cards and print other letters on several more cards. Have the children sit on the floor in a semicircle. Ask them to pretend that the floor in front of them is a big drum. Then hold up the cards, one at a time, and have the children beat on the floor with their hands whenever they see the letter D. Continue as long as interest lasts.

Variation: Provide the children with real drums or coffee cans that have plastic lids.

D Detective

Make a "detective hat" by labeling
a baseball cap with the letter *D*.
Print *D*'s and other letters on Post-it
brand notes and stick the notes
around the room where the children
can easily find them. Choose one
child to put on the hat and be the *D*
Detective. Have the detective walk
around the room and search for
"evidence of *D*." When the detective
finds a *D* note, have him or her
bring it back to you. Then choose
another child to be the *D* Detective.
Continue the game until everyone
has had a turn.

Doughnut Puzzles

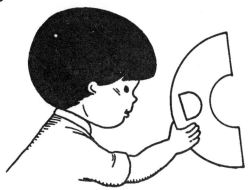

Cut large doughnut shapes (one for
every two children) from different
colors of construction paper. Cut
each shape into two puzzle pieces.
Mark one piece with an upper-case
D and the other with a lower-case *D*.

Give each of the children a doughnut half and have them note the
colors and the letters. Then let them
walk around to find the matching
halves of their doughnuts.

The Letter D

D's in the Dirt

Place a layer of dry dirt in a shallow box or pan. Print the letter D on an index card and attach the card to the box. Let the children take turns drawing D's in the dirt with their fingers.

D Is for Diamond

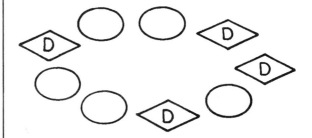

Cut large diamond and circle shapes out of construction paper. Print the letter D on each diamond. Tape the shapes to the floor in a circle. Then play music and let the children walk around on the shapes. When you stop the music, have the children who are standing on the diamonds raise their hands. Continue as long as interest lasts.

More Ideas for Fun With D

- Dance to music.
- Form D shapes with fingers.
- Draw doodles.
- Recite the nursery rhyme "Deedle, Deedle, Dumpling."
- Play with dolls in a doll house.
- Dust furniture.
- Be ducks, dogs, dinosaurs or donkeys and have a parade.
- Take turns opening the door for others.
- Celebrate a Dad's Day and invite fathers to attend.
- Play dress-up.

Put Some Doughnuts on the Dish
Sung to: "If You're Happy and You Know It"

Put some doughnuts on the dish, on the dish,
Put some doughnuts on the dish, on the dish.
Put some doughnuts on the dish,
Put as many as you wish.
Then say, "D is for the doughnuts on the dish."

Repeat, substituting other words that
begin with D for the word "doughnuts."

Elizabeth McKinnon

D Snacks

Give each child a small plate with a
paper doily placed on top. Set out
pitted dates and other dried fruits.
Let the children arrange small
amounts of the dried fruits on their
doily-covered plates to eat for
snacks.

Variation: Use a favorite recipe to
make dumplings.

Children's Books:
- *A Dark Dark Tale*, Ruth Brown, (Dial).
- *The Doorbell Rang*, Pat Hutchins, (Morrow).
- *Five Little Ducks*, Raffi, (Crown).
- *Have You Seen My Duckling?*, Nancy Tafuri, (Morrow).
- *A Visit From Dr. Katz*, Ursula Le Guin, (Macmillan).
- *Your Turn, Doctor*, Deborah Robison, (Dial).

The Letter D

Little Duck
Sung to: "Yankee Doodle"

Once there was a little duck
Who lived down by the lake.
His mother had to quack at him
'Cause he was always late.
Quack, quack, quack, quack, quack,
Hurry, don't be late.
Quack, quack, quack, quack, quack,
Don't make your mother wait.

Jean Warren

I'm Happy I'm a Doctor
Sung to: "My Bonnie Lies Over the Ocean"

I'm happy I'm a doctor,
I help to make people well.
I'm happy I'm a doctor,
It makes me feel just swell.
I'm a doctor,
I help to make people well, well, well.
I'm a doctor,
I'm happy, can't you tell?

Jean Warren

Contributors:

Jan Bodenstedt, Jackson, MI
Marilyn Dais Machosky,
    Westerville, OH

Alphabet Patterns

Use the patterns on the following pages to make stick puppets, learning games, alphabet books and other teaching aids.

duck

doctor

Dd

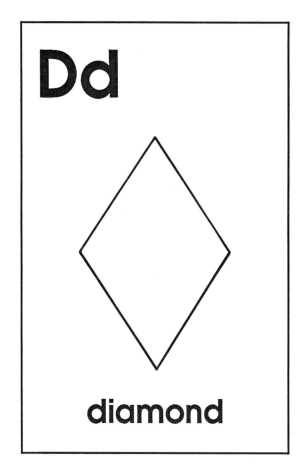

diamond

Dd

dinosaur

Dd

dog

Dd

doll

Dd

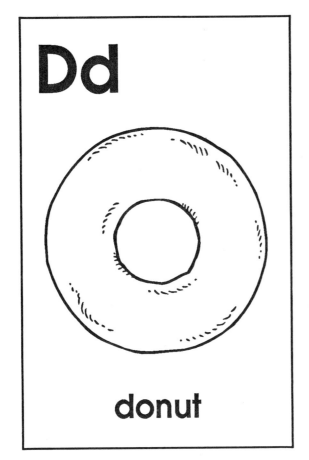

donut

Dd

door

Dd

drum

Dd

duck

The Letter E

Display/Play Box for *E*

Decorate a box with the letter *E* to use throughout your *E* unit. Inside the box place items (or pictures of items) whose names begin with *E*. Below are some suggestions.

- eagle
- earmuffs
- earphones
- earring
- easel
- egg
- egg beater
- elastic
- elephant
- elevator
- elf
- engine
- envelope
- eraser
- Eskimo

Eggshell *E*'s

Cut large letter *E* shapes out of heavy paper. Set out glue, cotton swabs and crushed eggshell pieces that have been rinsed and patted dry. Let the children glue the eggshell pieces on their letter shapes, using the cotton swabs as applicators.

Variation: If eggshells are not available, let the children attach egg stickers to their *E* shapes. Or have them glue on small egg shapes cut out of wrapping paper.

My *E* Book

Make a book for each child by stapling several pieces of white paper together with a construction paper cover. Print "My *E* Book" and the child's name on the front. Set out magazine pictures of things whose names begin with *E*, along with upper- and lower-case *E*'s cut from ads or article titles. Let the children choose the pictures and letters they want and glue them on their book pages. Later, arrange a time for the children to "read" their books to you.

Variation: Make books by cutting gray construction paper covers and white pages into elephant shapes. Or use white construction paper for the covers and cut the books into egg shapes.

E's in Eggs

Label stickers with *E*'s and attach them to large plastic eggs. Inside each egg put a picture of something whose name begins with *E*. Place the eggs in a basket. Have the children sit in a circle with the basket in the middle. Let each child in turn take an egg from the basket and name the letter on it. Then have the child open the egg and name the picture inside.

E Is for Elbows

Print the letter *E* on five or six index cards and print other letters on several more cards. Sit in front of the children and hold up the cards one at a time. Whenever the children see the letter *E*, have them bend their arms and move their elbows up and down.

The Letter E

E's in the Envelope

Print an upper-case *E* on the front of an envelope. Cut index cards in half. Print upper-case *E*'s on most of the cards and print other letters on the rest. Mix up the cards and place them in a pile. Let the children take turns sorting through the cards and placing those that are marked with *E* inside the envelope.

Variation: Label one envelope with an upper-case *E* and another envelope with a lower-case *E*. Print upper- and lower-case *E*'s on the index cards. Let the children take turns placing the cards in the appropriate envelopes.

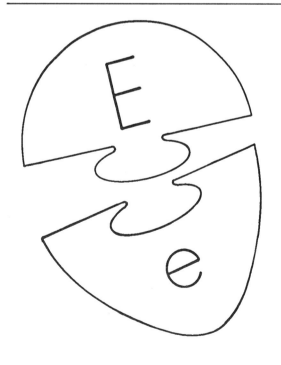

Egg Puzzles

Cut several large egg shapes out of posterboard. Cut each egg shape into two puzzle pieces. Print an upper-case *E* on the left-hand piece and a lower-case *E* on the right-hand piece. Then spread out the pieces on the floor and let the children have fun putting the egg puzzles together.

E Board Game

On a square of posterboard, trace around a Popsicle stick to make an upper-case *E* shape. Set out the posterboard square and four Popsicle sticks. Let the children take turns placing the Popsicle sticks on top of the tracings to form the letter *E*.

Variation: Use tongue depressors instead of Popsicle sticks.

Estimating

Place sets of colorful objects, such as marbles, jacks or golf tees, in separate recloseable plastic bags. Have the children sit in a circle. Pass one of the bags around the circle for the children to handle and examine. Give each child a chance to estimate how many objects are inside the bag. Write down the numbers for the group to see. Then empty the bag and count together the number of objects that were inside. Did anyone's estimate come close? Follow the same procedure with the other bags of objects.

The Letter E

Elephants Balancing

Arrange a long piece of string on the floor in a wide circle. Have the children line up by the circle and pretend to be elephants. Recite the rhyme below and let the first child in line start walking around on the string. Then have the second child start walking on the string as you repeat the rhyme, this time beginning with the words "Two little elephants balancing." Continue in the same manner until all the children are walking on the string. Then change the last line of the poem to read: "Now, no more elephants."

One little elephant balancing,
Step by step on a piece of string.
Oh, my — what a stunt!
Now, here comes another elephant.

Adapted Traditional

More Ideas for Fun With *E*

- Do easy exercises.
- Draw *E*'s on a chalkboard, then erase them.
- Form *E*'s on the floor with bodies.
- Count eleven eggs.
- Enjoy easel painting.
- Celebrate an Earth Day.
- Do simple science experiments.
- Glue pictures of *E* items on a giant *E* shape.
- Take pretend rides in an elevator or on an escalator.

E, E, What Do You See?
Sung to: "Skip to My Lou"

E, E, What do you see?

What do you see that starts with *E*?

I see an elf, that's what I see.

Hip, hip, hurray for *E*!

Repeat, substituting other words that start
with *E* for the word "elf." Set out items from
your *E* Display/Play Box (see page 46)
before singing the song.

Elizabeth McKinnon

Egg Snacks

Plan to serve eggs in a variety of
ways throughout your *E* unit. For
example, try scrambling, frying,
poaching and boiling eggs. Serve
hard-boiled eggs plain or sliced. Or
let the children help use them to
make egg salad or deviled eggs.

Children's Books:
- *Easter Bunny That Overslept,* Priscilla Friedrich, (Lothrop).
- *The Empty Pot,* Demi, (Holt).
- *Five Minutes' Peace,* Jill Murphy, (Putnam).
- *Fix-It,* David McPhail, (Dutton).
- *I Can Be an Electrician,* Dee Lillegard, (Children's Press).
- *Stand Back I'm Going to Sneeze,* (Morrow).

The Letter E

Did You Ever See an Elephant?
Sung to: "Did You Ever See a Lassie?

Did you ever see an elephant,
An elephant, an elephant,
Did you ever see an elephant
Spray water with her trunk?
Spray water all over,
Spray water all over.
Did you ever see an elephant
Spray water with her trunk?

Did you ever see an elephant,
An elephant, an elephant,
Did you ever see an elephant
Eat peanuts with her trunk?
Throw peanuts in her mouth,
Throw peanuts in her mouth.
Did you ever see an elephant
Eat peanuts with her trunk?

Susan A. Miller

I Am a Fine Electrician
Sung to: "My Bonnie Lies Over the Ocean"

I am a fine electrician,
I help to bring you light.
I hook up the wires to lamps,
I make your world so bright.
Light, light, light, light,
I help to bring you light, light, light.
Light, light, light, light,
I make your world so bright.

Jean Warren

Contributors:
Betty Ruth Baker, Waco, TX
Jan Bodenstedt, Jackson, MI
Susan A. Miller, Kutztown, PA

Alphabet Patterns
Use the patterns on the following pages to make stick puppets, learning games, alphabet books and other teaching aids.

elephant

electrician

Ee

eagle

Ee

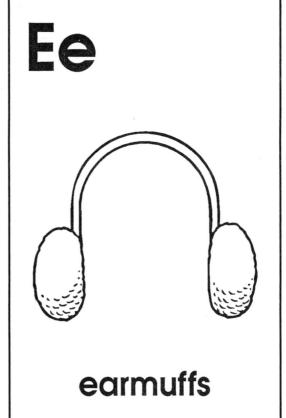

earmuffs

Ee

easel

Ee

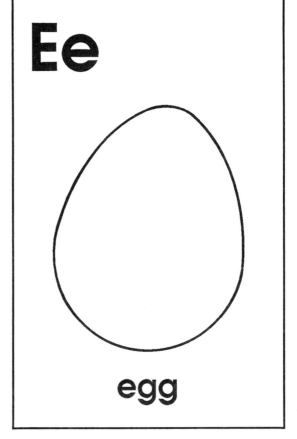

egg

Ee

eggplant

Ee

elephant

Ee

elf

Ee

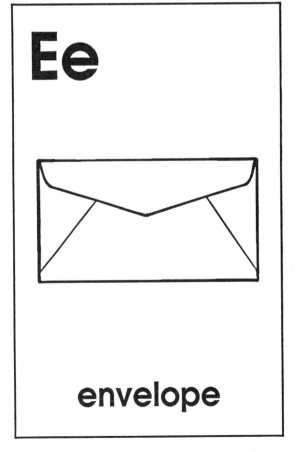

envelope

The Letter F

Display/Play Box for F

Decorate a box with the letter F to use throughout your F unit. Inside the box place items (or pictures of items) whose names begin with F. Below are some suggestions.

- fan
- farm
- feather
- felt
- fern
- fire engine
- fish
- flag
- flamingo
- flower
- flute
- fly
- football
- fork
- frog
- fur

Feather F's

Cut large letter F shapes out of heavy paper. Set out brushes, glue and small feathers. (Use white feathers from an old pillow or colored feathers purchased from a craft store.) Let the children brush glue on their letter shapes and arrange the feathers on top of the glue.

Variation: Instead of gluing on feathers, let the children dip their fingers into different colors of tempera paint and make fingerprints all over their F shapes.

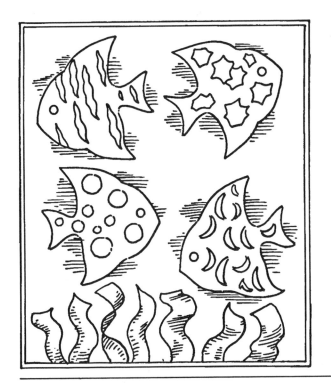

Far-Out Fish

Show pictures of tropical fish and discuss their shapes and colors. Give each child a construction paper fish shape. Set out glue and small scraps of colorful paper torn into various shapes. Invite the children to make "far-out fish" by gluing the paper scraps on their fish shapes any way they wish. Display the fish on a bulletin board with a blue background and add green crepe paper streamers for seaweed. Title the display "Far-Out Fish."

Fingerpainted Fans

Give each child a paper plate to use for the top part of a fan. Let the children fingerpaint on their plates, using any color they wish. Allow the plates to dry on a flat surface. Make a handle for each fan by gluing two tongue depressors together and slipping the edge of the paper plate between them. When the glue has dried, print the letter *F* on each fan. Then let the children have fun fanning their faces with their fingerpainted fans.

The Letter F

Feeling the Letter *F*

Make a bulletin board display of *F*'s cut from fake fur, felt, flannel and foil. Add a few upper-case *F*'s formed with long feathers, if desired. Invite the children to touch the letters and describe how they feel.

Found an *F*

Place items from your *F* Display/ Play Box (see page 56) on the floor. Have the children sit around the items in a circle. Let one child begin by choosing an item, holding it up and naming it. Then sing the song below, substituting the name of the item for "feather" and the child's name for "Jamie." Continue until each child has had a turn.

Sung to: "Found a Peanut"

Found a feather, found a feather,
Found a feather on the floor.
Jamie just now found a feather,
Found a feather on the floor.

Elizabeth McKinnon

Fee, Fi, Fo, Fum

Print the letter *F* on five or six index cards and print other letters on several more cards. Have the children sit in front of you. Begin by saying, "Fee, fi, fo, fum. When you see the letter *F*, wave your fingers just for fun." Then show the children the cards, one at a time, and have them wave their fingers whenever they see the letter *F*.

Fishing for *F*'s

Cut small fish shapes out of construction paper. Print the letter *F* on most of the shapes and print other letters on the rest. Attach a paper clip to each fish. Make a fishing pole by tying a piece of string to a yardstick or a wooden spoon. Tie a magnet on the end of the string. Set out a large shallow box for a pond. Label the box with the letter *F* and place the fish shapes inside it. Let each child have a turn catching a fish. If the fish is marked with the letter *F*, let the child keep it. If it is marked with another letter, have the child put it back into the pond and try again. Continue until each child has caught at least one *F* fish.

The Letter F

Follow the Footprints

Trace around the children's feet on pieces of colored construction paper. Cut out the footprint shapes, print *F*'s on them and cover them with clear self-stick paper. Tape the footprints to the floor to create pathways leading to the snack area, the art area, the bathroom, etc. Have the children follow the footprints as they move from one area to another.

Variation: Cut footprint shapes out of colored self-stick paper. Attach pairs of footprints to the floor in a simple pattern (two feet together, two feet apart, two feet together, etc.). Let the children follow the pattern by jumping from one set of footprints to the next.

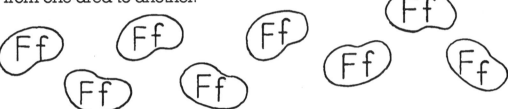

Fabulous Feelings

Have the children stand in a circle. Help them to act out feelings whose names begin with the letter *F*. Some examples would be feeling fabulous, feeling furious, feeling foolish, feeling funny, feeling full and feeling frisky.

More Ideas for Fun With *F*

- Float around like feathers.
- Fold fabric squares.
- Listen to fables or folktales.
- Pretend to play flutes or fiddles.
- Count the five fingers on each hand.
- Form *F*'s on the floor with bodies.
- Have fun saying "fiddlesticks!"
- Make funny faces.

There Are F's Everywhere
Sung to: "If You're Happy and You Know It"

There are F's everywhere, everywhere,
There are F's everywhere, everywhere.
Frogs and forks and feathers too,
And flags, to name a few.
There are F's everywhere, everywhere.

Repeat, substituting other words that
begin with F for the words "frogs,"
"forks," "feathers" and "flags."

Jean Warren

Fruit Faces

At snacktime set out small pieces of fruit, such as banana slices, orange segments, apple wedges, strawberries and grapes. Give each child a small paper plate. Let the children choose pieces of fruit and arrange them on their plates to create funny faces. Allow time for admiring the fruit faces before the children eat them.

Children's Books:
- *Clifford's Good Deeds*, Norman Bridwell, (Scholastic).
- *Firemouse*, Nina Barbaresi, (Crown).
- *Fish Is Fish*, Leo Lionnni, (Random House).
- *Jump, Frog, Jump!*, Robert Kalin, (Mulberry).
- *Seven Froggies Went to School*, Kate Duke, (Dutton).*
- *Story of Ferdinand*, Munro Leaf, (Viking).

The Letter F

Jump, Little Frog
Sung to: "Frere Jacques"

Jump, little frog; jump, little frog
To the pond, to the pond.
Catch a fly for dinner,
Catch a fly for dinner.
Yum, yum, yum! Yum, yum, yum!

Bonnie Woodard

Firefighter Song
Sung to: "Down by the Station"

Down at the firehouse
Early in the morning,
You can see our clothes
Hanging in a row.
When there is a fire,
We can dress real fast.
Boots, jackets, hats, gloves,
Off we go!

Jean Warren

Contributors:
Rita Galloway, Harlingen, TX
Marilyn Dais Machosky,
    Westerville, OH
Bonnie Woodard, Shreveport, LA

Alphabet Patterns
Use the patterns on the following pages to make stick puppets, learning games, alphabet books and other teaching aids.

frog

firefighter

Ff

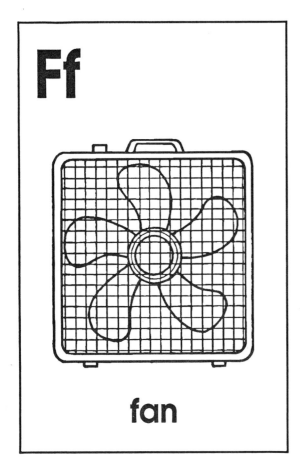

fan

Ff

feather

Ff

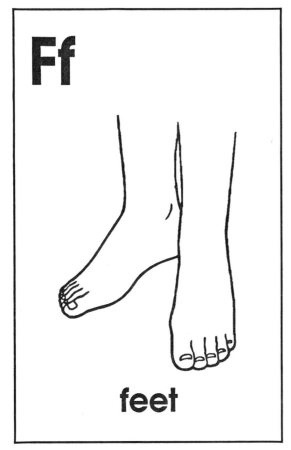

feet

Ff

fish

Ff

flag

Ff

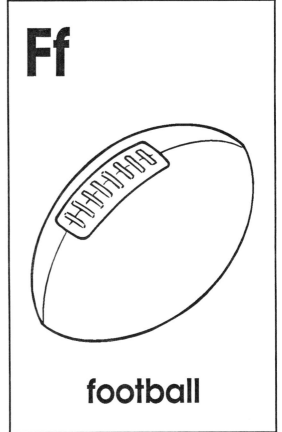

football

Ff

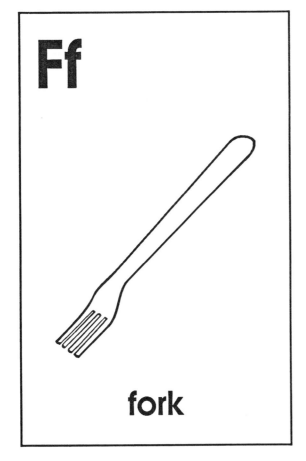

fork

Ff

frog

The Letter *F*   **65**

The Letter G

Display/Play Box for G

Decorate a box with the letter G to use throughout your G unit. Inside the box place items (or pictures of items) whose names begin with G. Below are some suggestions.

- garden
- gate
- giraffe
- glass
- globe
- glove
- glue
- goggles
- golf ball
- goose
- gorilla
- gourd
- grapes
- grass

Glitter G's

Cut large letter G shapes out of heavy paper. Let the children paint their letters green. Have them sprinkle green glitter all over the wet paint. Then help them shake off the excess glitter.

Variation: Have the children brush glue all over their G shapes. Then let them sprinkle on gold glitter.

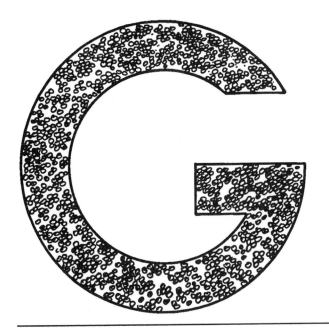

Gravel G's

Cut large letter G shapes out of cardboard. Brush glue on the letters and sprinkle on aquarium gravel (available at pet stores). When the glue has dried, invite the children to touch the letters and describe how they feel.

Variation: To create a different texture, cover the cardboard letters with globs of glue. Allow the glue to dry before setting out the letters.

G Collages

Print the letter G on pieces of light green construction paper. Set out glue and magazine pictures of items whose names begin with G. Give each child a 2-inch-wide strip of dark green construction paper and a pair of scissors. Let the children snip along the edges of their strips to create grass fringes. Have them glue their grass strips on their light green papers. Then let them choose pictures of other G items to add to their G collages.

The Letter G

Garbage Bag Guessing Game

Label a plastic garbage bag with the letter G. Have the children sit on the floor in a circle. Place several items from your G Display/Play Box (see page 66) in the middle of the circle and name each one with the group. Ask the children to close their eyes while you place one of the items inside the garbage bag. When they open their eyes, have the children try guessing which item is in the bag. Let the first child to guess correctly place a different item in the garbage bag for the next round of the game. Continue until each child has had a chance to hide a G item.

Variation: Pass the garbage bag around the circle and let the children try to identify the item inside by touch.

G Is for Graph

Make a graph by dividing a large piece of paper into two columns. Label the graph with the letter G. Draw a picture of green grapes at the top of one column and a picture of purple grapes at the top of the other. Hang the graph on a wall or an easel. Have the children take turns telling whether they prefer green grapes or purple grapes. After each child's response, draw a square in the appropriate column on the graph. When everyone has had a turn, count with the children the number of squares in each column. Compare and discuss the two groups using words such as these: "larger than, smaller than, more than, less than."

Extension: If desired, try graphing the number of "guys" and "gals" in the group.

A Garden of G's

Make a "garden" by filling a box with sand or dirt. Label the box with the letter G. Cut flower shapes from different colors of construction paper. Print G's on most of the shapes and print other letters on the rest. Attach the flower shapes to tongue depressors. Let the children sort through the shapes to find the G flowers. Then have them plant the flowers in the sand or dirt to create a "garden of G's."

Creating Green

Place small amounts of yellow and blue fingerpaint inside a recloseable plastic sandwich bag. Sit with the children in a circle. Pass the bag around and let each child rub it gently in his or her hands. When the bag gets back to you, hold it up and let the children observe the new color they created. Announce "G is for green!"

Grinning for G

Print the letter G on five or six index cards and print other letters on several more cards. Ask the children to sit in front of you. Then hold up the cards, one at a time, and have the children grin whenever they see the letter G.

The Letter G

Giggle Game

Ask one child to lie down on the floor. Have a second child lie down with his or her head on the first child's stomach. Have a third child lie down with his or her head on the stomach of the second child. Continue this pattern until all the children are lying on the floor. To play the game, have the first child start giggling. As he or she does so, have the second child start giggling, then the third child and so on. Let the children continue creating chain reactions of giggles as long as interest lasts.

Extension: If desired, tape record the children's giggles. Play back the tape later and see if the children can listen to it without giggling.

More Ideas for Fun With *G*

- Gallop to music.
- Celebrate a Green Day, a Gold Day or a Gray Day.
- Play "golf" with yardsticks and plastic golf balls.
- Have a growling, gobbling or grinning contest.
- Pretend to be ghosts and glide around the room.
- Sniff grass, garlic and gumdrops and describe their scents.

G Song

Sung to: "Twinkle, Twinkle, Little Star"

When I look around I see
Many things that start with G.
I see grass and girls galore,
I see gloves and so much more.
Won't you look around with me
And sing for things that start with G?

Repeat, substituting other words that begin with G for the words "grass," "girls" and "gloves." Have pictures of G items on hand while you sing the song.

Elizabeth McKinnon

G Snacks

For snacktime serve grapes or grape juice. Or use the recipe below to make gazpacho (chilled vegetable soup).

Gazpacho — In a blender mix together the following ingredients: 2 ripe tomatoes, 1/4 green bell pepper, peeled cucumber, 1/4 cup chopped 1/2 onion, one 6-ounce can tomato juice, 1 tablespoon lemon juice and a dash of garlic powder. Chill for several hours. Makes 4 to 5 small servings.

Children's Books:

- *Adventure of Albert the Running Bear*, Barbara Isenberg, (Houghton Mifflin).
- *The Ghost-Eye Tree*, Bill Martin, (Viking).
- *The Goat and the Rug*, Charles Blood, (Macmillan).
- *Goggles*, Ezra Jack Keats, (Macmillan).
- *Nanny Goat and the Seven Little Kids*, Eric Kimmel, (Holiday House).
- *Patchwork Cat*, William Mayne, (Random House).

The Letter G

My Silly Billy Goat
Sung to: "The Wheels on the Bus"

My silly billy goat
Eats the clothes off the line,
The clothes off the line,
The clothes off the line.
My silly billy goat
Eats the clothes off the line,
As soon as I hang them up.

My silly billy goat
Eats the shirts and the pants,
The shirts and the pants,
The shirts and the pants.
My silly billy goat
Eats the shirts and the pants
As soon as I hang them up.

Let the children create additional verses by naming other articles of clothing to replace "shirts" and "pants."

Susan A. Miller

I Am a Garbage Collector
Sung to: "My Bonnie Lies Over the Ocean"

I am a garbage collector,
I pick up the bags and the cans.
I help keep our city clean,
And that makes a cleaner land.
Land, land, land, land,
I help make a cleaner land, land, land.
Land, land, land, land,
I help make a cleaner land.

Jean Warren

Contributors:

Betty Ruth Baker, Waco, TX
Jan Bodenstedt, Jackson, MI
June Crow, Weaverville, NC
Marilyn Dais Machosky,
   Westerville, OH
Susan A. Miller, Kutztown, PA

Alphabet Patterns

Use the patterns on the following pages to make stick puppets, learning games, alphabet books and other teaching aids.

goat

garbage collector

Gg

gate

Gg
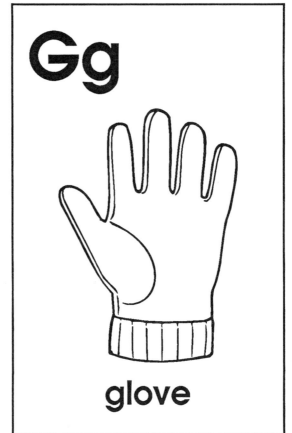

glove

Gg

goat

Gg

goose

Gg

gorilla

Gg

grapes

Gg

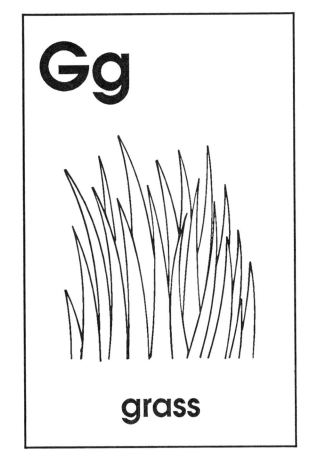

grass

Gg

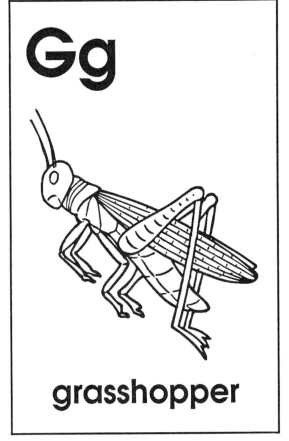

grasshopper

Display/Play Box for *H*

Decorate a box with the letter *H* to use throughout your *H* unit. Inside the box place items (or pictures of items) whose names begin with *H*. Below are some suggestions.

- hammer
- handkerchief
- handle
- hanger
- harmonica
- hat
- hay
- heart
- helicopter
- hen

- hippopotamus
- holly
- honey
- hoop
- horn
- horse
- hose
- hot dog
- house

Heart *H*'s

Cut large letter *H* shapes out of heavy paper. Cut small heart shapes from wallpaper, wrapping paper and various colors of construction paper. Let the children glue the hearts all over their *H* shapes. If desired, let them also attach a few heart stickers.

H's in the House

Decorate a box to look like a house and print the letter *H* on the front. Cut index cards in half. Print *H*'s on most of the cards and print other letters on the rest. Let the children take turns sorting through the cards and placing those that are marked with *H* inside the house.

H's in the Hat

Label a large hat with the letter *H*. Have the children sit in a circle. Place the hat in the middle of the circle, along with pictures of things whose names begin with *H* or small objects from your *H* Display/Play Box (see page 76). Let each child have a turn choosing a picture or an object, naming it and then placing it in the hat. When the hat is full, let each child remove an item and say, "*H* is for _____."

Variation: Hide *H* items under the hat while the children close their eyes. Have the children take turns guessing what is hidden under the hat.

H Is for Hands

Cut out small magazine pictures of things whose names begin with *H*. Help each child trace around his or her hand on a piece of construction paper. Have the children cut out their hand shapes (or cut them out yourself). Then let each child choose a picture of an *H* item to glue on the palm of his or her hand shape. If desired, use the decorated hands to make a bulletin board trim.

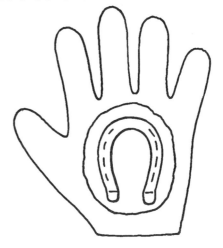

The Letter H

Horses and Hurdles

Set out several plastic horses. Let the children help build hurdles by placing rectangular wooden blocks on the floor in *H* shapes. Then let the children have fun "jumping" the horses over the hurdles.

Extension: Make hurdles for the children to jump by placing such objects as pillows, ropes or chalkboard erasers on the floor. Arrange the objects in *H* shapes, if desired.

Heart Match-Ups

Cut several heart shapes out of construction paper. Cut each heart lengthwise into two puzzle pieces. Print an upper-case *H* on the left half of each heart puzzle and glue it on a separate square of posterboard. Print lower-case *H*'s on the right halves of the puzzles and place them in a pile. Spread out the posterboard squares on the floor. Let the children take turns choosing puzzle pieces from the pile and matching them to the puzzle pieces on the posterboard squares.

Color Hats

Cut a clown face out of white felt and use felt scraps or felt-tip markers to make hair and facial features. Then cut one clown hat shape each from the following colors of felt: red, yellow, blue, purple, white, green, brown. Cut an additional hat shape out of orange felt and add black decorations. Place the clown face on a flannelboard. Then read the poem below and let the children help put the appropriate hats on the clown's head.

My name, boys and girls, is Carl the
   Clown.
I wear my hats all over town.

Each one has its own color name,
Which you can learn if you play my
   game.

Oh, here's a hat, and it is red.
It fits so nicely on my head.

Now when I wear my hat of yellow,
I'm told I'm quite a dandy fellow.

I hope you like my hat of blue.
I'll put it on now, just for you.

My purple hat is just for good.
I'd wear it always if I could.

I wear a white hat on a sunny day.
It looks quite nice, my friends all say.

I put on my green hat to go to the
   park,
But I take it off when it gets dark.

And when it's dark, I put on brown.
This hat is for a sleepy clown.

My orange and black hat is for
   Halloween night.
Yes, indeed, I'm quite a sight!

Susan M. Paprocki

The Letter H

Hula-Hoop Fun

Bring in a Hula-Hoop and use it for various activities. For example, place the Hula-Hoop on the floor and let the children toss beanbags inside of it, walk around it in different ways or hop in and out of it. Or have the children sit around the Hula-Hoop for circle games or stand inside it when taking turns for show and tell. If desired, demonstrate the "right way" to use the Hula-Hoop and let the children give it a try.

Human *H*'s

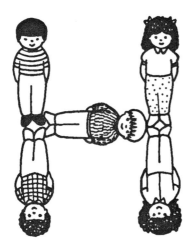

Let five children at a time create a "human *H*" on the floor. To form each side of the *H*, have two children lie on their backs with their feet touching. Have the remaining child stretch out between the two sides to form the crossbar.

More Ideas for Fun With *H*

- Play horns or harmonicas.
- Celebrate a Hat Day.
- Hunt for *H*'s that have been hidden around the room.
- Go on a hike.
- Listen to one another's heartbeats.
- Graph hair colors.
- Play Drop the Handkerchief.
- Fly around like helicopters.
- Have a group hug.

H Makes Me Happy
Sung to: "Twinkle, Twinkle, Little Star"

H is for hair and *H* is for hand,
H is for heels on which we stand.
H is for houses here and there,
H is for hats seen everywhere.
H is for hearts and for horses too,
H makes me happy, how about you?

Elizabeth McKinnon

H Snacks

Serve hamburgers for snacktime. Or let the children help make ham sandwiches. Before the children eat, ask, "Is everyone hungry?"

Children's Books:
- *Big Orange Spot*, Daniel Pinkwater, (Scholastic).
- *Bored Nothing to Do*, Peter Spier, (Doubleday).
- *The Boy Who Was Followed Home*, Margaret Mahy, (Dial).
- *Hot Air Henry*, Mary Calhoun, (Morrow).
- *Hot Hippo*, Mwenye Hadithi, (Little Brown).
- *A House Is a House for Me*, Mary Ann Hoberman, (Viking).

The Letter H

H-I-P-P-O
Sung to: "Old MacDonald Had a Farm"

Here's an animal you should know,
H-I-P-P-O.
She eats a lot of vegetables,
H-I-P-P-O.
She's very big, her skin is gray,
She likes to swim in the water all day.
Here's an animal you should know,
H-I-P-P-O.

Debra Lindahl

I Am a House Painter
Sung to: "Hokey-Pokey"

I put my paintbrush in,
I take my paintbrush out,
I put my paintbrush in,
Then I brush it on a house.
I am a house painter,
And I paint inside and out.
That's what my job's about.

Jean Warren

Contributors:
Betty Ruth Baker, Waco, TX
Jan Bodenstedt, Jackson, MI
Rita Galloway, Harlingen, TX
Debra Lindahl, Libertyville, IL
Betty Silkunas, Lansdale, PA

Alphabet Patterns
Use the patterns on the following pages to make stick puppets, learning games, alphabet books and other teaching aids.

hippopotamus

house painter

The Letter *H*   **83**

Hh

hamburger

Hh

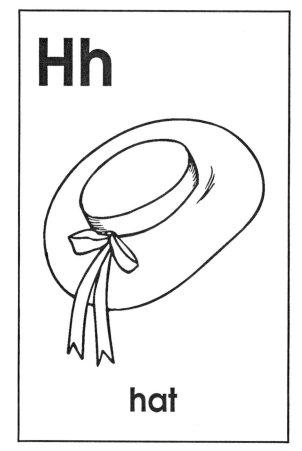

hat

Hh

heart

Hh

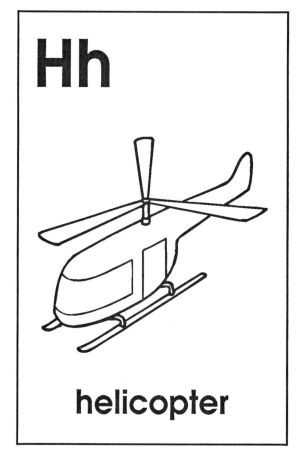

helicopter

Hh

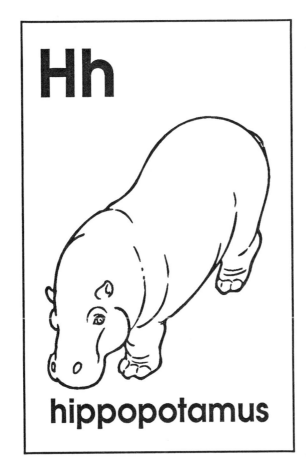

hippopotamus

Hh

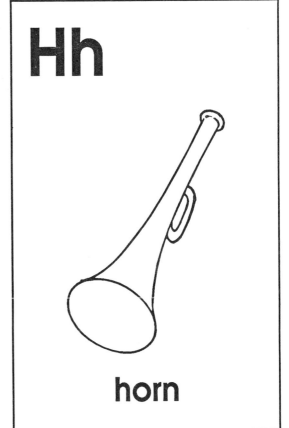

horn

Hh

horse

Hh

house

The Letter I

Display/Play Box for *I*

Decorate a box with the letter *I* to use throughout your *I* unit. Inside the box place items (or pictures of items) whose names begin with *I*. Below are some suggestions.

- ice cream container
- ice cube tray
- ice skates
- icicle
- igloo
- iguana
- Indian
- infant
- ink
- insects
- iris
- iron
- ironing board
- island
- ivy

Insect *I*'s

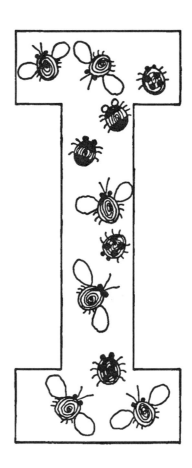

Cut large letter *I* shapes out of heavy paper. Set out inkpads and fine-line felt-tip markers. Have the children press their fingers on the inkpads and make fingerprints all over their letter shapes. Then let them turn their fingerprints into insects by adding eyes, legs, wings and other details with the felt-tip markers.

My *I* Book

Make a book for each child by stapling several pieces of white paper together with a construction paper cover. Print "My *I* Book" and the child's name on the front. Set out magazine pictures of things whose names begin with *I*, along with upper- and lower-case *I*'s cut from ads or article titles. Let the children choose the pictures and letters they want and glue them on their book pages. Later, arrange a time for the children to "read" their books to you.

Variation: Make books by cutting white construction paper covers and white pages into igloo shapes.

Inkblots

Give each child a piece of white construction paper. Let the children squeeze drops of colored ink or food coloring on their papers. Help them fold their papers in half. Have them gently rub across their papers and then unfold them to reveal the ink-blot designs they created. Encourage the children to tell what they think their inkblots look like. Then cut out the designs and use them to make a bulletin board display titled "*I* is for Inkblots."

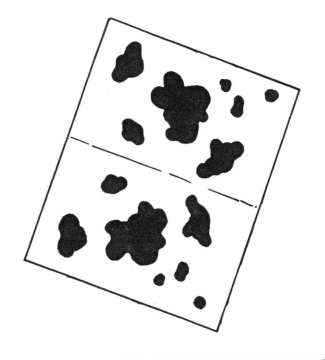

The Letter I

Ice Cream Cone Game

Cut several ice cream cone shapes out of brown felt. Use a felt-tip marker to print the letter *I* on the shapes. Then place the cones on a flannelboard. Cut circles from different colors of felt to represent scoops of ice cream. Print *I*'s on most of the circles and print other letters on the rest. Place the circles near the flannelboard. Let the children take turns selecting the scoops of ice cream that are marked with *I* and placing them above the cone shapes to create single- or multi-decker ice cream cones.

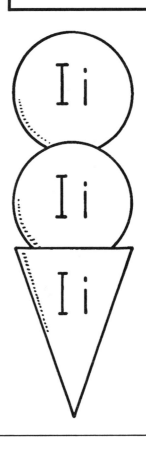

I Is for In

Have the children sit on the floor in a circle. Place your *I* Display/Play Box (see page 86) in the middle of the circle, along with a basket and a paper bag. Let the children take turns removing the *I* items from the box, naming them and placing them on the floor. Then give directions such as these: "Put the ice cube tray in the bag; Put the ice skates in the basket; Put the iron in the box." Continue until every child has had a turn.

Lower-Case *I*'s

Make a number of lower-case *I*'s by cutting rectangles and circles out of colored construction paper. Give each child several sets of the shapes, along with a sheet of plain white paper. Let the children arrange the rectangles and circles on their papers to form lower-case *I*'s. Then let them glue the shapes to their papers, if desired.

Variation: Let the children use strips of plastic tape and self-stick dots to create lower-case *I*'s.

Incredible *I*'s

Divide the children into groups of threes. Have the children in each group lie on the floor and form an upper-case *I* with their bodies. Then have the children trade places and form new letter *I*'s.

How Many Inches?

Show the children a ruler or a yardstick and point out the inch marks. Use the ruler to measure such things as a pencil, a piece of yarn or a finger. Then hang a piece of butcher paper on a wall and have the children stand in front of it. Mark each child's height on the paper. Measure the child's height in inches and write the number, along with the child's name, above his or her mark. When you have finished, discuss how many inches tall each child is.

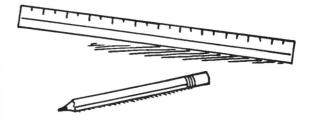

The Letter I

In and Out the Igloo

Stand with the children in a wide circle to form an "igloo." Then sing the song below with the children and act out the movements described. Continue singing the song until each child has had a turn going "in and out the igloo."

Sung to: "In and Out the Window"

Go in and out the igloo,
   (One child weaves in and out of the circle.)
Go in and out the igloo,
Go in and out the igloo,
Go in and out once more.

   (Child returns to place in circle.)

Let's all walk round the igloo,
   (Everyone joins hands and circles round.)
Let's all walk round the igloo,
Let's all walk round the igloo,
Let's all walk round once more.

Adapted Traditional

More Ideas for Fun With *I*

- Crawl like inchworms.
- Make ice cubes.
- Make illustrations for a group story.
- Iron doll clothes with a toy iron.
- Play musical instruments.
- Glue pictures of *I* items on a giant *I* shape.
- Take turns introducing one another by name.
- Create imaginary insects with collage materials.
- Make initial necklaces.

I Is Such a Simple Letter

Sung to: "Twinkle, Twinkle, Little Star"

I is such a simple letter,
There's no other that I like better.
I stands for me when I want it to,
I is for ink and for ice cream too.
I is such a simple letter,
There's no other that I like better.

Repeat, substituting other words that begin
with *I* for the words "ink" and "ice cream."

Elizabeth McKinnon

Ice Cream

In a clean 13-ounce coffee can mix together 1 cup milk, 1 cup whipping cream, ½ cup unsweetened frozen apple juice concentrate, thawed, and ¾ teaspoon vanilla. Put on the lid and place the can inside a clean 34-ounce coffee can. Fill the remaining space in the large can with ice and cover the ice with rock salt. Put on the lid and place the can on the floor. Roll the can back and forth for 10 minutes. Open up both cans. Scrape down the insides of the smaller can and stir in 1 cup fresh or frozen strawberries, mashed. Replace the small lid. Pour the excess water out of the large can and add more ice and rock salt. Put the large lid back on and roll the cans for 5 to 7 minutes more until the ice cream hardens. Serve immediately or freeze until later. Makes 8 small servings.

Children's Books:

- *The Book of Foolish Machinery*, Donna Pape, (Scholastic).
- *Christina Katerina & the Box*, Patricia Gauch, (Putnam).
- *Iggy*, Marcia Newfield, (Houghton Mifflin).
- *I'm Gonna Tell Mama I Want an Iguana*, Tony Johnston, (Putnam).
- *The Important Book*, Margaret Wise Brown, (Harper).
- *Ira Sleeps Over*, Bernard Waber, (Houghton Mifflin).

The Letter I

Oh, Once I Met an Iguana

Sung to: "My Bonnie Lies Over the
   Ocean"

Oh, once I met an iguana
Who was big and ugly and gray.
He looked just like a big lizard,
And this is what he did say:
"Glug, glug, glug, glug,
Come and give me a hug, hug, hug.
Glug, glug, glug, glug,
Won't somebody give me a hug?"

He sat all day on a rock,
Under the hot, hot sun.
He looked so sad and lonely,
No wonder he wanted a hug.
Hug, hug, hug, hug,
I went and gave him a hug, hug, hug.
Hug, hug, hug, hug,
I went and gave him a hug!

Jean Warren

I'm An Inventor

Sung to: "Three Blind Mice"

Inventor, inventor,
Always dreaming of something more.
I like to invent things that are new,
I like to invent things that I can do
Helpful tasks for me and you.
Inventor.

Jean Warren

Contributors:

Barbara Dunn, Hollidaysburg, PA
Carole Hardy, Pittsburgh, PA

Alphabet Patterns

Use the patterns on the following
pages to make stick puppets, learning games, alphabet books and
other teaching aids.

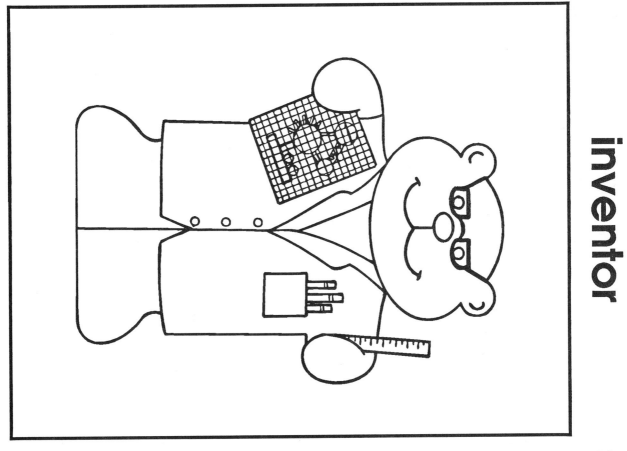

iguana

inventor

The Letter *I*   **93**

Ii

ice cream cone

Ii

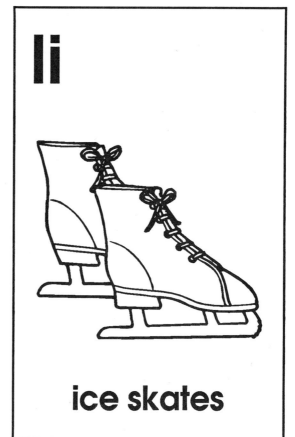

ice skates

Ii

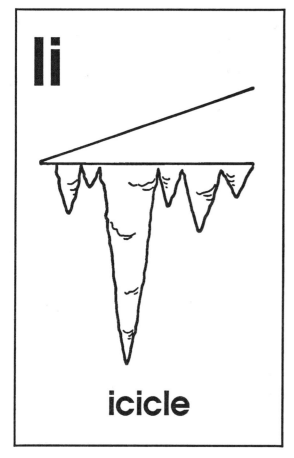

icicle

Ii

igloo

Ii

ink

Ii

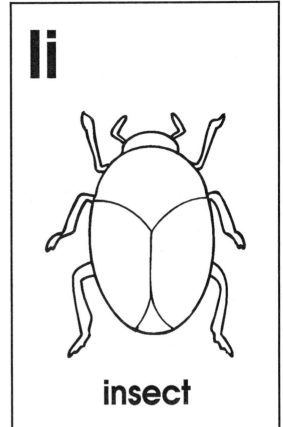

insect

Ii

iron

Ii

island

The Letter J

Display/Play Box for J

Decorate a box with the letter J to use throughout your J unit. Inside the box place items (or pictures of items) whose names begin with J. Below are some suggestions.

- jacket
- jack-in-the-box
- jack-o'-lantern
- jam
- jar
- jeans
- jeep
- Jell-O
- jelly
- jellybeans
- jet
- jewels
- juice
- jump rope

Jewelry J's

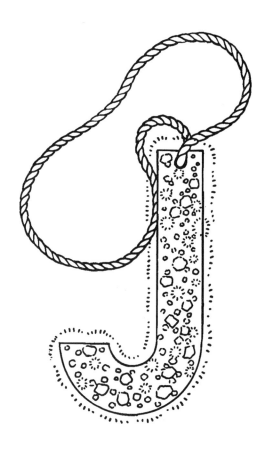

Give each child a 6-inch-tall J shape cut from posterboard. Have the children decorate their letters by gluing on such materials as glitter, small beads, sequins or foil scraps. Punch holes in the tops of the letter shapes. Then tie on loops of yarn or colored cord and let the children wear their "jewelry J's" as necklaces.

A Journey to Japan

I am taking a journey to Japan,
My jet is leaving in June.
I am packing up my J things,
You'd think I was off to the moon.

I am taking a jack-o'-lantern
And plenty of juice and Jell-O.
Of course, I will take my jewelry
And my jacket that's sort of yellow.

I am planning to take my jellyfish,
Who speaks perfect Japanese.
He taught me how to jitterbug,
Jeepers, that jars the knees!

I packed a jigsaw puzzle
And a book about how to juggle.
I didn't forget my jack rabbit,
The bed toy I love to snuggle.

Now I'll just pack my jump rope
And a jar of jam, if I can.
Then I think I'll have all my J things
For my journey to Japan.

Susan M. Paprocki

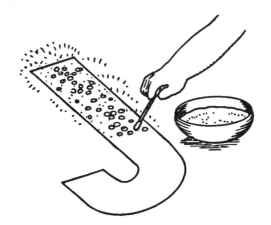

Jewel J's

Cut large letter *J* shapes out of heavy paper. Set out cotton swabs, sequins and shallow containers of glue. Let the children glue the sequins all over their letter shapes, using the cotton swabs as applicators.

The Letter J

Judging Juice

Give each child two small paper cups. Pour grape juice into one cup and orange juice into the other (or use any two flavors desired). As the children sip their juice, ask them to judge which kind tastes best. Then take a vote to see which juice is the winner.

Extension: Graph the children's responses on a large piece of paper. Ask questions such as these: "Which juice received the most votes? Which juice received the least votes? Which juice did most people like the best? The least?"

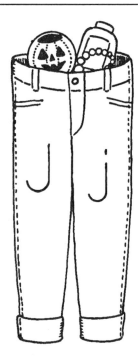

J's in the Jeans

Label an old pair of jeans with the letter *J* and stitch or tie the ends of the legs closed. Inside the jeans place pictures of things whose names begin with *J* or small objects from your *J* Display/Play Box (see page 96). Have the children sit around the jeans in a circle. Let them take turns removing an item from the jeans, naming it and placing it on the floor. When all the items have been removed, give directions such as these: "Put the jet inside the jeans; Put the jump rope inside the jeans; Put the jar inside the jeans."

Jogging for *J*

Print the letter *J* on five or six index cards and print other letters on several more cards. Have the children stand in front of you. Then hold up the cards, one at a time, and have the children jog in place each time they see the letter *J*.

Variation: Have the children jump instead of jog.

Jellybeans in Jars

Set out two wide-mouthed jars. Label one jar with an upper-case *J* and the other with a lower-case *J*. Cut jellybean shapes out of different colors of construction paper. Print upper-case *J*'s on half of the shapes and print lower-case *J*'s on the other half. Then mix up the jellybean shapes and let the children take turns sorting them into the appropriate jars.

The Letter J

Let's Jump for *J* Today
Sung to: "When Johnny Comes Marching Home"

Let's jump and jump for *J* today, hurray, hurray!
Let's jump and jump for *J* today, hurray, hurray!
Let's jump for jackets seen here and there,
Let's jump for jeans seen everywhere.
Oh, let's jump, jump, jump, jump, jump for *J* today!

Repeat, substituting other words that begin
with *J* for the words "jackets" and "jeans."

Elizabeth McKinnon

J Is for Jazz

Play jazz recordings and let the
children dance and sway to the
music. If desired, show pictures of
musical instruments used to play
jazz. Have the children pretend to
play the instruments along with the
recordings.

More Ideas for Fun With *J*

- Do jumping jacks.
- Recite the nursery rhyme "Jack Be Nimble."
- Make a *J* on the floor with a jump rope and walk around the letter as it is written.
- Do jigsaw puzzles.
- Trace around a cane to make *J*'s.
- Pretend to be jockeys or jugglers.
- Find the jacks in a deck of playing cards.
- Smile like jack-o'-lanterns.

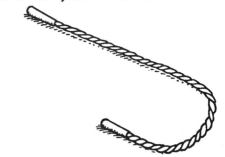

Jack-In-The-Box Fingerplay

Recite the poem below with the children and let them act out the movements described.

Jack-in-the-box,
You sit so still.
   (Close fist with thumb inside.)
Won't you come out?
Yes, I will!
   (Pop out thumb.)

Traditional

Variation: Have the children crouch down near the floor. Then recite the poem and have them jump up at the end.

Jam Snack

Give each child one or two strawberries on a small plate. Have the children cut up their strawberries and mash them with forks. Then let the children spread peanut butter on slices of warm wheat toast and top them with their strawberry "jam."

Children's Books:

- *Clean Enough*, Kevin Henkes, (Morrow).
- *Hey, Al*, Arthur Yorinks, (FS&G).
- *Johnny Appleseed*, Steven Kellogg, (Morrow).
- *Jumanji*, Chris Van Allsburg, (Houghton Mifflin).
- *Junglewalk*, Nancy Tafuri, (Morrow).

The Letter J

The Jaguar Has Black Spots
Sung to: "The Farmer in the Dell"

The jaguar has black spots,
The jaguar has black spots.
His coat is yellow and he's a fast fellow.
The jaguar has black spots.

The jaguar lives in the forest,
The jaguar lives in the forest.
He's like a cat, only bigger than that.
The jaguar lives in the forest.

Jean Warren

I Am a Janitor
Sung to: "The Mulberry Bush"

This is the way I sweep the floors,
Sweep the floors, sweep the floors.
This is the way I sweep the floors,
I am a janitor.

This is the way I mop the halls,
Mop the halls, mop the halls.
This is the way I mop the halls,
I am a janitor.

This is the way I wash the windows,
Wash the windows, wash the windows.
This is the way I wash the windows,
I am a janitor.

This is the way I take out the trash,
Take out the trash, take out the trash.
This is the way I take out the trash,
I am a janitor.

Jean Warren

Contributors:
Karen Seehusen, Ft. Dodge, IA
Betty Silkunas, Lansdale, PA

Alphabet Patterns
Use the patterns on the following pages to make stick puppets, learning games, alphabet books and other teaching aids.

jaguar

janitor

Jj

jack-in-the-box

Jj

jack-o'-lantern

Jj

jacks

Jj

jar

Jj

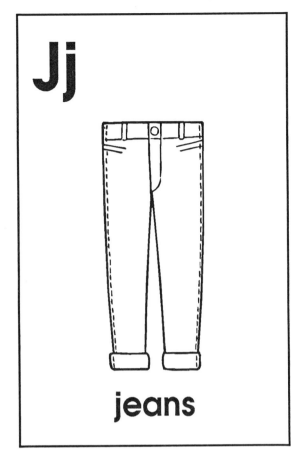

jeans

Jj

jeep

Jj

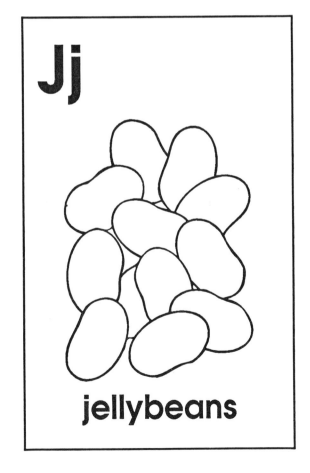

jellybeans

Jj

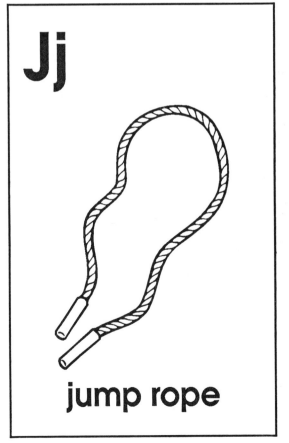

jump rope

The Letter K

Display/Play Box for K

Decorate a box with the letter K to use throughout your K unit. Inside the box place items (or pictures of items) whose names begin with K. Below are some suggestions.

- kaleidoscope
- kangaroo
- ketchup
- kettle
- key
- kimono
- king
- kitchen
- kite
- kitten
- kiwi fruit
- koala

Kernel K's

Cut large letter K shapes out of heavy paper. Set out small bowls of popcorn kernels. Have the children cover their letter shapes with glue or paste. Then let them place the kernels on top of the glue

Sorting K's

Select ten lined index cards. Print upper-case K's on five of the cards and lower-case K's on the other five. Make sure that the letters are printed in the proper proportions. Mix up the cards and let the children take turns sorting them into two piles.

Kindness Collage

Print "K is for Kindness" at the top of a piece of butcher paper. Let the children look through magazines to find pictures that show people being kind to one another or doing kind things. Have the children tear or cut out the pictures and glue them on the butcher paper. Display the kindness collage on a wall or a bulletin board and encourage the children to talk about the pictures.

Extension: Purchase stickers that depict friendship or kindness. When you observe a child being kind to another, mention it and attach a kindness sticker to his or her shirt.

Key Chain

Cut several key shapes out of posterboard. On each shape glue a small picture (or a sticker) of something whose name begins with K. Print the letter K on the shape also. Punch a hole in the top of each key shape and fasten the shapes together with a key chain. Give the keys to the children and let them take turns naming the letters and pictures on them.

The Letter K

K's in the Kettle

Label a large kettle that has a lid with the letter *K*. Have the children sit on the floor in a circle. Place the kettle in the middle of the circle, along with pictures of things whose names begin with *K* or small objects from your *K* Display/Play Box (see page 106). Name each of the *K* items with the group. Then have the children close their eyes while you place one of the items in the kettle and put on the lid. When the children open their eyes, have them try guessing which item is hidden inside the kettle. Let the first child to guess correctly hide an item for the next round of the game. Continue until each child has had a chance to hide a *K* item.

Kicking Games

Take the children outside and let them have fun kicking different kinds and sizes of balls around. Have them try kicking the balls forward, backward and up into the air. If desired, provide additional objects for the children to kick, such as rolled-up socks or bags stuffed with crumpled newspaper.

K Is for Kings

Put together a deck of playing cards that includes the kings from several decks. Let the children sort through the cards to find the kings. If desired, have them place the red kings in one pile and the black kings in another. Store the cards in a box labeled with the letter K.

Hint: To make the game simpler, you may wish to remove the queens and the jacks from the deck.

Kangaroo Pouch Game

Draw a large picture of a kangaroo on a piece of posterboard. Cut a pocket shape from fabric and staple it to the kangaroo picture for a pouch. Title the picture "K is for Kangaroo" and hang it on a wall at the children's eye level. Cut index cards into small squares. Print K's on most of the squares and print other letters on the rest. Spread out the cards on a table or on the floor. Let the children take turns selecting squares that are marked with K and placing them inside the kangaroo's pouch.

The Letter K

Kite, Kite

Have the children pair up. In each pair let one child pretend to be a kite and the other child pretend to be the kite flyer. Sing the song below and have the kite flyers pretend to hold the kite strings as their kites act out the movements described. Then have the children trade places and sing the song again.

Sung to: "Twinkle, Twinkle, Little Star"

Kite, kite, soaring high,
Reaching, reaching to the sky.
First you're high, then you're low,
Swooping, swirling, round you go.
Kite, kite, fine and free,
Dancing, dancing, just for me.

Susan M. Paprocki

We Say *K*'s OK
Sung to: "Old MacDonald Had a Farm"

There is a letter we all know,
And its name is *K*.
K is a letter that we like,
We say *K*'s OK.
K is for king, *K* is for key,
K is for all the kites we see.
There is a letter we all know,
And its name is *K*.

Repeat, substituting other words that begin with *K* for the words "king" and "kites."

Elizabeth McKinnon

Kabobs

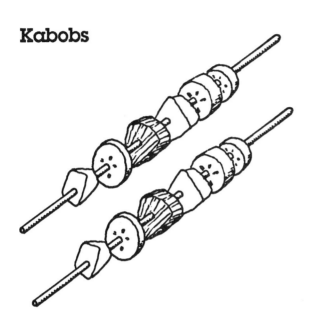

Let the children use plastic knives to cut such fruits as apples, bananas and pineapple rings into chunks. Include kiwi fruit and kumquats, if available. Help the children thread the fruit chunks on wooden skewers to create kabobs. Serve the kabobs at snacktime.

Note: Have the children remove the fruit chunks from their skewers before eating.

More Ideas for Fun With *K*

- Look through a kaleidoscope.
- Play kazoos.
- Make crowns and be kings for the day.
- Pretend to be kittens.
- Form *K*'s on the floor with bodies.
- Create a kitchen area for dramatic play.
- Name foods that taste good with ketchup.
- Demonstrate some karate moves.
- Blow kisses.

Children's Books:

- *Katy No-Pocket*, Emmy Payne, (Houghton Mifflin).
- *Kermit the Hermit*, Bill Peet, (Houghton Mifflin).
- *Koala Lou*, Audrey Wood, (Harcourt).
- *Norma Jean, Jumping Bean*, Joanna Cole, (Random House).

The Letter K

Oh, I'm a Kangaroo
Sung to: "The Farmer in the Dell"

Oh, I'm a kangaroo,
I live down at the zoo.
I like to jump around a lot.
How about you?

Oh, I'm a kangaroo,
I live down at the zoo.
I carry a baby in my pouch.
How about you?

Jean Warren

I Am a Karate Instructor
Sung to: "The Farmer in the Dell"

I am a karate instructor,
I wear a suit of white.
I show you how to protect yourself
And how to move just right.

I show you how to stand,
I show you how to defend.
I show you how to jump and yell
And let your body bend.

Jean Warren

Contributors:
Jan Bodenstedt, Jackson, MI

Alphabet Patterns
Use the patterns on the following pages to make stick puppets, learning games, alphabet books and other teaching aids.

kangaroo

karate instructor

Kk

kangaroo

Kk

ketchup

Kk

kettle

Kk

key

Kk

king

Kk
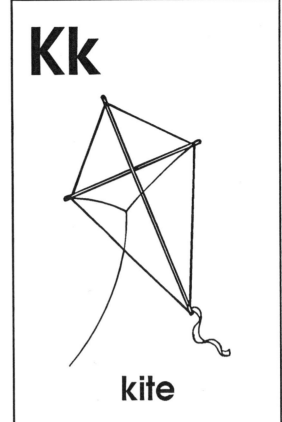
kite

Kk

kitten

Kk

koala

The Letter L

Display/Play Box for L

Decorate a box with the letter L to use throughout your L unit. Inside the box place items (or pictures of items) whose names begin with L. Below are some suggestions.

- lace
- ladder
- ladle
- ladybug
- lamb
- lamp
- lantern
- leaf
- leash
- lemon
- letter
- lettuce
- lid
- lime
- lion
- lizard
- lobster
- lock
- locket
- log

Laced L's

Cut large letter L shapes out of posterboard. Use a hole punch to punch holes around the edges of the shapes. Tie a long piece of yarn through one of the holes in each shape. Wrap tape around the loose ends of the yarn pieces to make "needles." Let the children lace the yarn through the holes around their posterboard letters. Then trim the loose yarn ends and tape them to the backs of the letter shapes.

Room Decorations for *L*

- Cut *L*'s from paper lace and attach them to a bulletin board.

- Cut circles out of different colors of construction paper. Attach straws to the circles to make lollipop decorations. Print *L*'s on the lollipops. Or let the children glue on pictures of things whose names begin with *L*.

- Have the children draw pictures showing love. Use the pictures to make an "*L* is for Love" bulletin board display.

L Collage

Use two pieces of long narrow paper to make a giant upper-case *L* as shown in the illustration. Place the paper *L* on a table or on the floor. Set out magazine pictures of things whose names begin with *L*, along with *L*'s cut from ads or article titles. Let the children work together to glue the pictures and letters on the giant *L*. Then display the *L* collage on a wall or a bulletin board.

Extension: Set out straws and straw halves. Let the children add to their collage by gluing on the straws in upper-case *L* shapes.

The Letter L

L's in Laps

Have the children sit on chairs in a circle. Place your L Display/Play Box (see page 116) in the middle. Let one child begin by choosing an item from the box, naming it and taking it back to his or her chair. Then sing the song below for the child, substituting the name of the item for the word "leaf" and the child's name for "Ashley." Continue until every child has had a turn.

Sung to: "If You're Happy and You Know It"

Put the leaf in your lap, in your lap,
Put the leaf in your lap, in your lap.
Put the leaf in your lap,
Then everybody clap
For the leaf Ashley has in her lap.

Elizabeth McKinnon

Leaf Game

Label a bushel basket or a box with the letter L. Cut leaf shapes out of construction paper. Print L's on most of the shapes and print other letters on the rest. Spread out the leaves on the floor and place the bushel basket nearby. Play music and let the children dance around. When you stop the music, have each child pick up a leaf. If the leaf is marked with L, have the child place it in the bushel basket. If the leaf is marked with another letter, have the child put it back on the floor. Continue until every child has had a chance to place at least one L leaf in the basket.

Like a Lion

Ask the children to pretend that they are lions roaming through the jungle. Then give the following directions: "Look around like a lion; Listen like a lion; Leap like a lion; Laugh like a lion; Lie down like a lion." If desired, play some jungle music while the children are doing their lion movements.

Variation: Let the children pretend to be lambs instead of lions.

Sorting the Laundry

Cut clothing shapes out of construction paper. Print *L*'s on some of the shapes and print other letters on the rest. Place the shapes in a basket. Let the children take turns sorting through the "laundry" and placing the shapes marked with *L*'s in one pile and the shapes marked with other letters in another pile. If desired, hang up a clothesline and let the children clip on the *L* clothing shapes with clothespins.

Leg Twist

Print large upper- and lower-case *L*'s on a long piece of butcher paper, spacing them out evenly. Let one child place one foot on an upper-case *L* and the other foot on a lower-case *L*. Have the first child remain standing in place as a second child locates an upper- and a lower-case *L* to stand on. Continue until all the children are standing on the butcher paper. The more children that are involved in the game, the more giggles and unusual positions there will be.

The Letter L

Five Little Ladybugs

Print *L*'s on red self-stick dots. Attach five of the dots to the fingers of each child's right or left hand to represent ladybugs. As you read the poem below, have the children wiggle one finger at a time, starting with their thumbs. At the end of the poem, have them "fly" their ladybugs away.

Five little ladybugs sitting in a tree,
The first one said, "I'm glad I'm me."
The second one said, "I feel great too."
The third one said, "How about you?"
The fourth one said, "It's time to fly away."
The fifth one said, "We'll talk another day."
Z-o-o-o-m!

Rita Galloway

More Ideas for Fun With *L*

- Play Leapfrog.
- Lift left hands, then left feet.
- Take turns being the line leader.
- Pick up litter and throw it in a trash can.
- Explore the color and scent of lavender.
- Print with different kinds of lids.
- Sing a lullaby.

I Love to Sing for the Letter *L*
Sung to: "Deck the Halls"

I love to sing for the letter *L*,
La-la-la-la-la, la-la-la-la.
I like the things that *L* can tell,
La-la-la-la-la, la-la-la-la.
Light the lamp and lick the lollipop,
La-la-la, la-la-la, la-la-la.
I just love the letter *L*,
La-la-la-la-la, la-la-la-la.

Bobbie Lee Wagman

Lettuce Lunch

Set out two or more different kinds of lettuce. Let the children wash the leaves and pat them dry with paper towels. Have them tear the lettuce into small pieces and place them in a large salad bowl. Make a lemon vinaigrette dressing by whisking together 6 tablespoons vegetable oil, 2 tablespoons lemon juice and $\frac{1}{4}$ teaspoon salt. Toss the lettuce with the lemon dressing and serve in small bowls.

Children's Books:

- *Dandelion*, Don Freeman, (Viking).
- *The Grouchy Ladybug*, Eric Carle, (Harper Row).
- *Happy Lion*, Louise Fatio, (Scholastic).
- *I Took My Frog to the Library*, Eric Kimmel, (Viking).
- *Little Old Lady Who Was Not Afraid of Anything*, Linda Williams, (Harper).
- *Walter's Magic Wand*, Eric Houghton, (Orchard).

The Letter L

I'm a Lion
Sung to: "Three Blind Mice"

I'm a lion, I'm a lion,
Hear me roar, hear me roar.
I love to sleep out in the sun,
And chase other animals just for fun,
In all the jungle I'm Number One.
I'm a lion.

Jean Warren

Librarian Song
Sung to: "Yankee Doodle"

All the boys and girls can come
And take home books for free.
I help them find books that they like
At the library.
I'm a librarian,
I check out the books.
Come and visit me real soon
And give my books a look.

Jean Warren

Contributors:
Jan Bodenstedt, Jackson, MI
Rita Galloway, Harlingen, TX
Marilyn Dais Machosky,
 Westerville, OH
Bobbie Lee Wagman, Milton, WI

Alphabet Patterns
Use the patterns on the following pages to make stick puppets, learning games, alphabet books and other teaching aids.

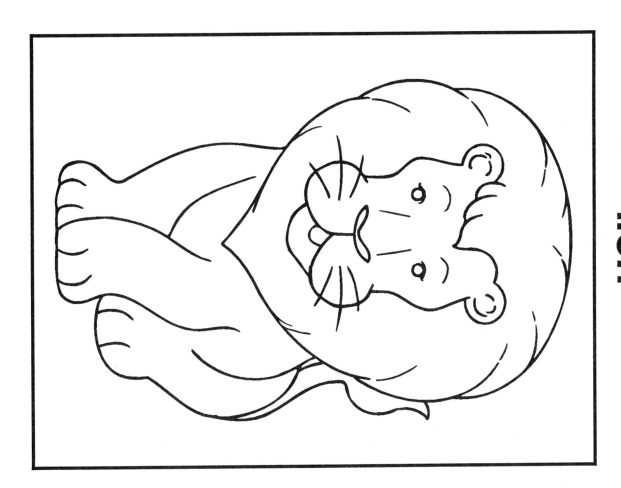

lion

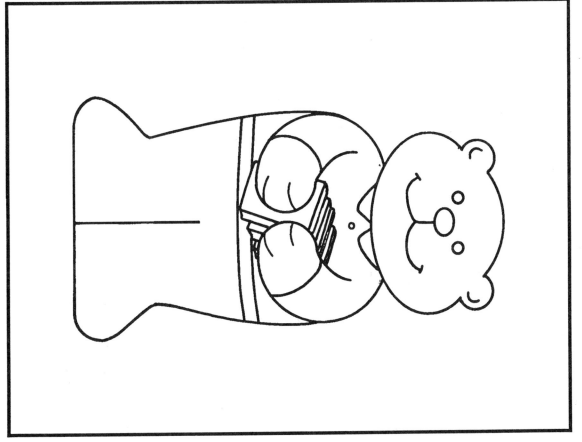

librarian

Ll

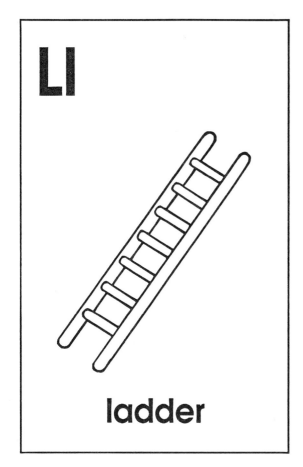

ladder

Ll

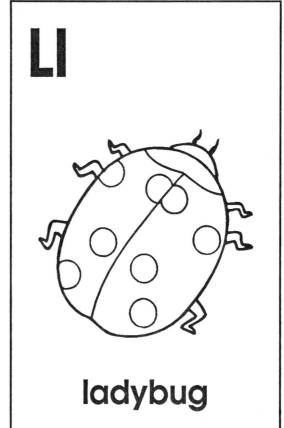

ladybug

Ll

lamb

Ll

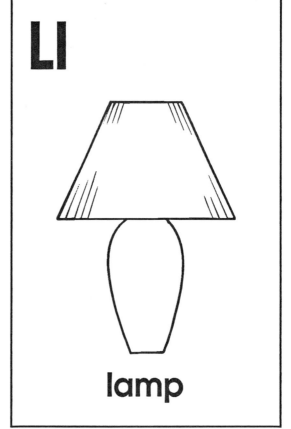

lamp

Ll

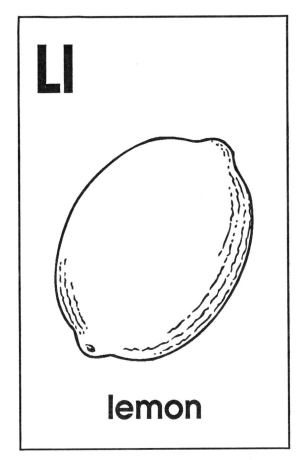

lemon

Ll

lion

Ll

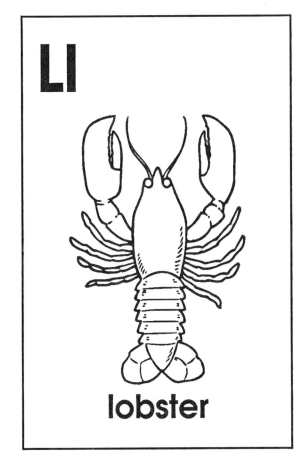

lobster

Ll

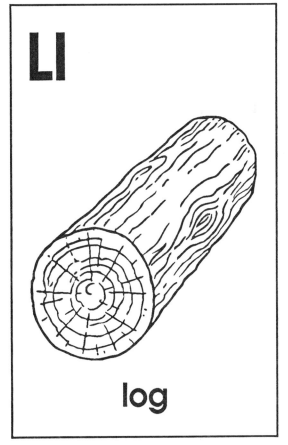

log

The Letter M

Display/Play Box for *M*

Decorate a box with the letter *M* to use throughout your *M* unit. Inside the box place items (or pictures of items) whose names begin with *M*. Below are some suggestions.

- macaroni
- magazine
- magnet
- magnifying glass
- mailbox
- map
- maraca
- mask
- milk carton
- mirror
- mitten
- monkey
- monster
- moon
- mop
- motorcycle
- mouse
- muffin tin
- music box

Macaroni *M*'s

Cut large letter *M* shapes out of heavy paper. Set out glue, brushes and small bowls of macaroni. Let the children brush glue on their letters. Then have them arrange pieces of macaroni on top of the glue.

Making Moons

Make paint pads by placing folded paper towels in shallow containers and pouring on small amounts of white tempera paint. Give each child a piece of black construction paper and a cork. Let the children make moon prints by pressing the ends of their corks on the paint pads, then on their papers. While the children are working, read the poem below out loud.

Moon, moon,
Up so high,
Big white moon
In the pitch black sky.

Moon, moon,
Mighty one,
Following soon
The setting sun.

Susan M. Paprocki

Mail Carrier Game

Place a large mailbox on a table. (Or use a cardboard carton decorated to resemble a mailbox.) Label the mailbox with the letter *M*. On the floor place objects from your *M* Display/Play Box (see page 126). Choose one child to be the Mail Carrier. Have the child walk around the *M* objects as everybody chants: "Mail Carrier, Mail Carrier, can you say? What will you put in our mailbox today?" Have the Mail Carrier pick up an object, name it, then take it to the mailbox and place it inside. Continue until every child has had a turn being the Mail Carrier.

Extension: Let the children take turns reaching into the mailbox and trying to identify the objects inside by touch.

Variation: Print *M*'s and other letters on the fronts of sealed envelopes. Spread out the envelopes on the floor. Let the children select the "*M* mail" to place in the mailbox.

The Letter M

M Mobile

Cut upper- and lower-case *M*'s out of construction paper or posterboard. Mix up the letters and spread them out on a table. Let each child walk by the table and choose one upper- and one lower-case *M*. Have the children decorate their letters with felt-tip markers. Punch a hole in each letter. Then tie the letters to a coat hanger with thread or yarn to create an *M* mobile. (Use more than one coat hanger, if necessary.) Hang the mobile from the ceiling or in a window.

Monkey See, Monkey Move

Print *M*'s on five or six index cards and print other letters on several more cards. Have the children stand in front of you. Show them the cards one at a time. Whenever they see the letter *M*, have them move about like monkeys.

Magnetic *M*'s

Attach metal paper clips to pictures of things whose names begin with *M*. Attach plastic paper clips to pictures of things whose names begin with other letters. Spread out the pictures on the floor. Let the children use a magnet to search for the pictures of things whose names begin with *M*. Have the children name the *M* pictures as they find them.

Mitten Match-Up

Have the children sit on the floor in a circle. Give them each a different colored or patterned mitten to put on one hand. Place the mates to the mittens in the middle of the circle. Let the children search through the pile to find their matching mittens and put them on their other hands.

Variation: Instead of using real mittens, cut pairs of mitten shapes from different colored or patterned paper. Print the letter *M* on the mitten shapes.

Mountains of *M*'s

Use a felt-tip marker to draw continuous *M* "mountains" on a long piece of butcher paper. Let the children trace over the *M* mountains with their fingers. Then let each child trace over the *M* mountains with a different colored felt-tip marker.

Extension: If desired, let the children glue magazine pictures of things whose names begin with *M* on the mountains.

Musical Chairs

Place a chair for each child in a circle, facing out. Tape a picture of an item whose name begins with *M* to the back of each chair. Sing the song below as you lead the children around the circle. At the end of the song, have each child stand by a chair and name the pictured item taped to it before sitting down. Continue playing the game as long as interest lasts.

Sung to: "The Farmer in the Dell"

Let's march around the chairs,
Let's march around the chairs.
March, marching one by one,
Let's march around the chairs.

Betty Silkunas

More Ideas for Fun With *M*

- Make masks or magic wands.
- Do marble painting.
- Mop the floor with a dry mop.
- Talk through a megaphone.
- Hold hands with partners to form *M*'s.
- Listen to a music box.
- Draw moustaches on pictures of faces cut from magazines.
- Grow mold on a damp piece of bread.
- Explore with mirrors and magnifying glasses.
- Make mudpies.

The *M*'s Are Marching
Sung to: "When Johnny Comes Marching Home"

The *M*'s are marching round the room, hurray, hurray!
The *M*'s are marching round the room in a big parade.
A monkey, a mouse, a mitten and more,
All are marching round the floor.
Oh, we're all so glad that they could come today!

Let three children at a time hold *M* items as
you sing and march around in a circle.
Substitute the names of the items for the
words "monkey," "mouse" and "mitten."

Jean Warren

M Meal
At snacktime serve the children a mixed-up menu of meat, mangoes, melons, and milk. If desired, let them spread margarine on bread slices and use the meat to make sandwiches. Then let them sit down and enjoy their "*M* meal."

Children's Books:
- *Caps for Sale*, Esphyr Slobodkina, (Scholastic).
- *Curious George*, H. A. Rey, (Houghton Mifflin).
- *Madeline's Rescue*, Ludwig Bemelmans, (Viking).
- *Mike Mulligan and His Steam Shovel*, Virginia Lee Burton, (Houghton Mifflin).
- *Mr. Griggs' Work*, Cynthia Rylant, (Orchard).
- *Post Office Book*, Gail Gibbons, (Harper).

The Letter M

I'm a Little Monkey
Sung to: "I'm a Little Teapot"

I'm a little monkey in the tree,
Swinging by my tail so merrily.
I can leap and fly from tree to tree,
I have lots of fun, you see.

I'm a little monkey, watch me play,
Munching on bananas every day.
Lots of monkey friends to play with me,
We have fun up in the tree.

Carla C. Skjong

Mail Carrier Song
Sung to: "My Bonnie Lies Over the Ocean"

I get to sort the mail,
Then carry it to your home.
The mail comes from all over,
Like New York, Paris and Rome.
Mail, mail, mail, mail,
I love to deliver the mail, mail, mail.
Mail, mail, mail, mail,
I love to deliver the mail.

Jean Warren

Contributors:
Jan Bodenstedt, Jackson, MI
Betty Silkunas, Lansdale, PA
Carla C. Skjong, Tyler, MN

Alphabet Patterns
Use the patterns on the following pages to make stick puppets, learning games, alphabet books and other teaching aids.

monkey

mail carrier

Mm

mailbox

Mm

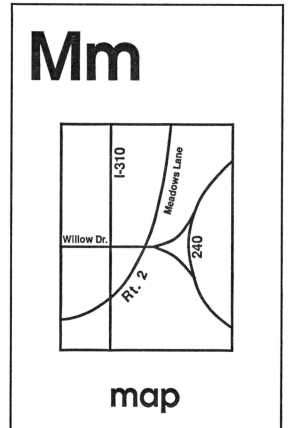

map

Mm

marbles

Mm

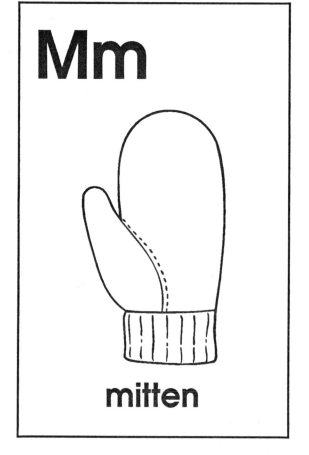

mitten

Mm

monkey

Mm

moon

Mm

mountain

Mm

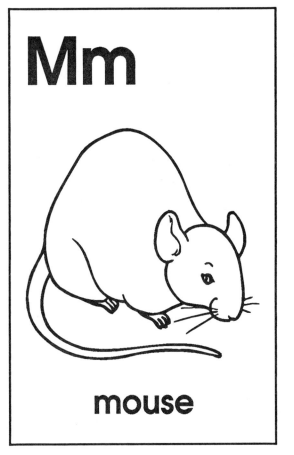

mouse

The Letter N

Display/Play Box for *N*

Decorate a box with the letter *N* to use throughout your *N* unit. Inside the box place items (or pictures of items) whose names begin with *N*. Below are some suggestions.

- napkin
- necklace
- necktie
- nest
- net
- newspaper
- nickel
- nightgown
- noodles
- numbers
- nutcracker
- nuts

Noodle *N*'s

Cut large letter *N* shapes out of heavy paper. Let the children brush glue on their letters. Then have them arrange noodles on top of the glue.

Variation: Let the children glue pieces of broken nutshells all over their letter shapes.

Naming N's

Have the children sit on the floor in a circle. In the middle place items from your N Display/Play Box (see page 136). Give clues about the different items and have the children try guessing their names. For example, for a nut you might say, "I see something small and brown that has a hard shell. Who can name it?" Continue until all the items have been named. If desired, repeat the game and let the children give the clues.

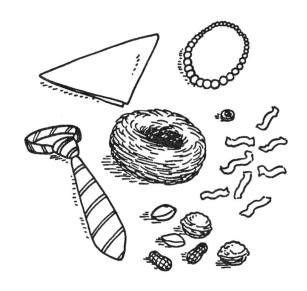

Newspaper N's

Collect the comics sections from newspapers. Give each child one comics page and a felt-tip marker. Have the children search for N's on their newspaper pages and circle them with their felt-tip markers. If desired, provide each child with an index card that has an upper- and lower-case N printed on it to use as a reference.

Nodding for N

Print the letter N on five or six index cards and print other letters on several more cards. Have the children sit on the floor in front of you. Hold up the cards one at a time. Whenever the children see the letter N, have them nod their heads.

The Letter N

Nut Number Necklaces

Cut several nut shapes for each child out of brown construction paper. Punch a hole in the top of each shape. Hide the nut shapes around the room and let the children hunt for them. (Make sure that each child finds some nuts.) When the hunt is over, have each child in turn bring his or her nut shapes to you. Count the number of shapes with the child, then write that number on one of the shapes. String the nut shapes on a piece of yarn to make a nut number necklace for the child to wear.

Net *N*'s

Glue nylon netting (available at fabric stores) to squares of posterboard. When the glue has dried, cut the squares into *N* shapes. Display the net *N*'s on a wall or a bulletin board and invite the children to trace over them with their hands.

Variation: Attach the net *N*'s to a tabletop with loops of tape rolled sticky sides out. Let the children place sheets of paper on top of the textured letters and rub over them with crayons.

N Neckties

Cut necktie shapes out of construction paper. Print the letter *N* in the center of each shape. Let the children decorate their neckties by brushing on glue and then sprinkling on glitter. When the glue has dried, punch holes in the tops of the neckties and tie on loops of yarn. Let the children wear their neckties like necklaces.

Whose Nose?

Cut large pictures of faces out of magazine ads. Cover the face pictures with clear self-stick paper. Use a craft knife to cut out the noses. Set out the noses and the pictures. Then let the children have fun trying to match the noses to the faces.

N Is for Nail

Set out blocks of scrap wood. Let one child at a time select a wood block and bring it to you. Use a hammer to start pounding a large nail into the wood block. Then let the child continue pounding the nail until it is firmly in place. If desired, print "*N* is for Nail" on the wood blocks and let the children take them home.

The Letter N

N Song
Sung to: "Ten Little Indians"

N is for nine and *N* is for noodles,
N is for nine and *N* is for noodles,
N is for nine and *N* is for noodles.
Let's count nine noodles now.

One little, two little, three little noodles,
    (Count out noodles one at a time.)
Four little, five little, six little noodles,
Seven little, eight little, nine little noodles.
Nine little noodles now.

Continue with similar verses, substituting such objects as napkins, nickels or nuts for noodles.

Elizabeth McKinnon

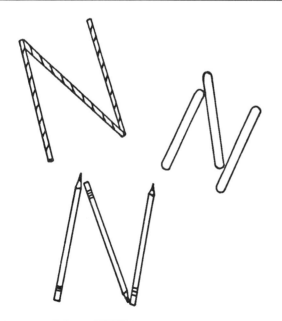

More Ideas for Fun With *N*

- Recite favorite nursery rhymes.
- Form *N*'s with straws, pencils or Popsicle sticks.
- Sew with plastic needles.
- Move like stiff dry noodles, then like limp cooked noodles.
- Crack open nuts with a nut cracker.
- Talk about nests made by birds, insects and animals.
- Take a nature walk around the neighborhood.

N Snacks

Let the children eat noodles or nuts at snacktime. Or let them help make nachos (see recipe below). Provide the children with napkins to use while they nibble on their *N* snacks.

Nachos — Have the children break hard taco shells into small pieces and sprinkle on grated cheese. Place the nachos on a cookie sheet and bake at 350 degrees until the cheese is hot and bubbly. Cool before serving.

Children's Books:

- *A Hospital Story*, Sara Stein, (Walker).
- *Just Awful*, Alma Whitney, (Harper).
- *Nightgown of the Sullen Moon*, Nancy Willard, (Harcourt).
- *Owl Moon*, Jane Yolen, (Putnam).
- *Owliver*, Robert Kraus, (Simon and Schuster).
- *There's a Nightmare in My Closet*, Mercer Mayer, (Dial).

The Letter N

Little Night Owl
Sung to: "Yankee Doodle"

Once there was a night owl
Who lived up in a tree.
He could often spot things
That others couldn't see.
Little night owl, answer me,
What do you see,
As you sit alone at night
Up in the tree?

I'm a little night owl
Who lives up in a tree.
I can often spot things
That others cannot see.
Once I saw a satellite
Passing over me,
As I sat alone at night
Up in the tree.

Repeat, letting the children suggest other
things that the night owl might have seen.
For example: "Once I saw a little moth
flying right by me; Once I saw a little
mouse run right under me."

Jean Warren

I'm a Nurse
Sung to: "Little White Duck"

I'm a nurse dressed in white,
And I feel just swell.
When you are sick,
I help to make you well.
I give you shots,
And if you're afraid,
I fix you up with a big Band-Aid.
I'm a nurse dressed in white,
And I feel just swell.
Now you're well!

Jean Warren

Contributors:
Betty Ruth Baker, Waco, TX
Jan Bodenstedt, Jackson, MI
Fawn Bostick, Allentown, PA

Alphabet Patterns
Use the patterns on the following
pages to make stick puppets, learning games, alphabet books and
other teaching aids.

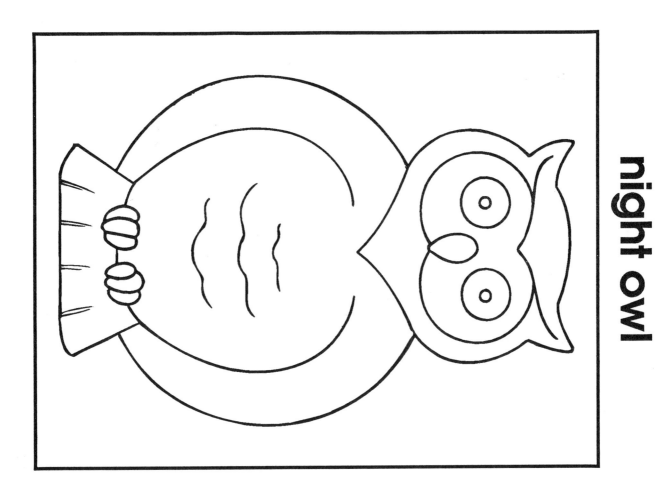

night owl

nurse

Nn

nail

Nn

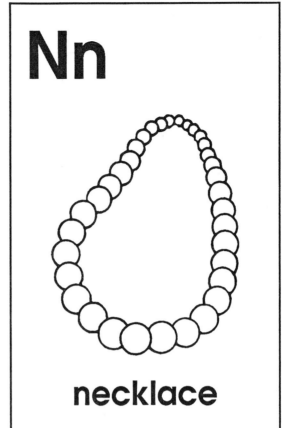

necklace

Nn

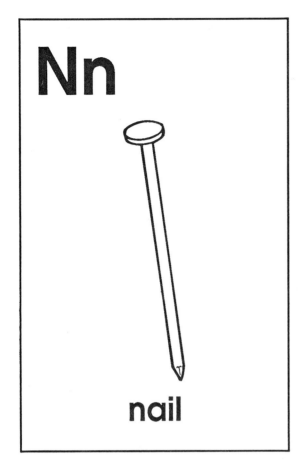

necktie

Nn

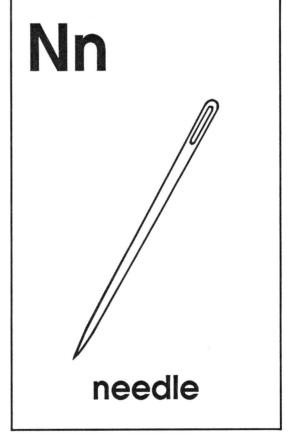

needle

Nn

nest

Nn

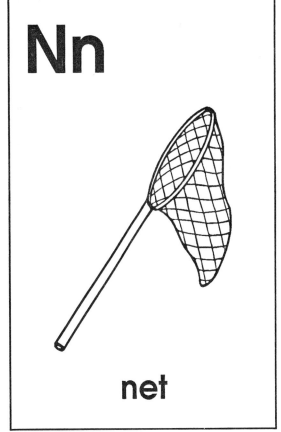

net

Nn

newspaper

Nn

nuts

The Letter O

Display/Play Box for O

Decorate a box with the letter O to use throughout your O unit. Inside the box place items (or pictures of items) whose names begin with O. Below are some suggestions.

- oar
- oatmeal box
- octopus
- oil
- olives
- onion
- orange
- ornament
- ostrich
- otter
- oval
- oven
- overalls
- owl
- ox
- oyster shell

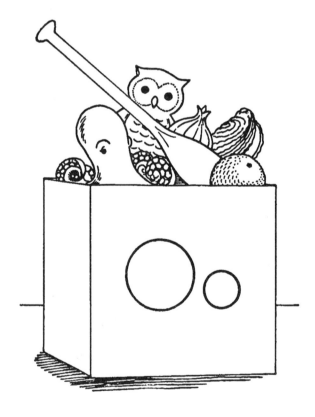

"O" O's

Cut large letter O shapes out of heavy paper. Set out self-stick reinforcement circles (available at stationery stores). Let the children stick the reinforcement circles all over their letter shapes to represent O's.

Variation: Have the children make orange fingerpaint designs on sheets of white paper. When dry, cut the papers into O shapes and display them around the room.

My *O* Book

Make a book for each child by stapling several pieces of white paper together with a construction paper cover. Print "My *O* Book" and the child's name on the front. Set out magazine pictures of things whose names begin with *O*, along with upper- and lower-case *O*'s cut from ads or article titles. Let the children choose the pictures and letters they want and glue them on their book pages. Later, arrange a time for the children to "read" their books to you.

Variation: Make books by cutting orange construction paper covers and white pages into round orange shapes. Or use green construction paper for the covers and cut the books into olive shapes. Glue a red oval at the top of each olive cover, if desired.

Printing *O*'s

Pour different colors of tempera paint into shallow containers. Set out construction paper and objects with round open ends, such as cardboard toilet tissue tubes, drinking straws, margarine tubs and plastic bottles. Invite the children to print *O*'s of various colors and sizes by dipping the open ends of the objects into the paint and pressing them on their papers.

The Letter O

Ollie the Octopus

Use butcher paper to create a large octopus body and eight tentacles. Attach the octopus to a wall or a bulletin board, making sure that the tentacles are spread out over a fairly large area. Print "Ollie the Octopus" on the octopus body and add facial features. Set out pictures of things whose names begin with O. Let each child in turn choose a picture and name it. Then help the child attach the picture to one of Ollie's tentacles. When all the pictures have been attached, name them together with the children.

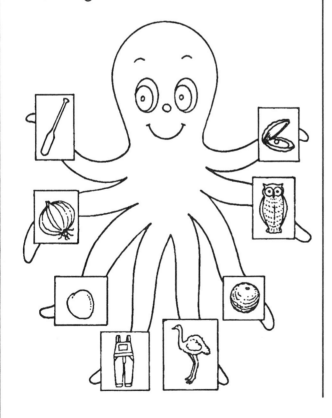

Orange Tree Game

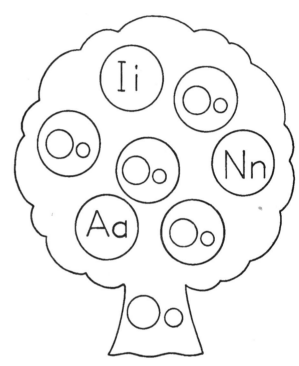

Cut a large tree shape out of felt and use a felt-tip marker to print the letter O on the trunk. Place the tree on a flannelboard. Cut circles out of orange felt for oranges. Print O's on most of the oranges and print other letters on the rest. Place the oranges on the felt tree. Then let the children take turns picking all the oranges that are not marked with O's.

Variation: Place all the felt oranges in a pile. Let the children take turns selecting the oranges that are

On and Off

Review the concepts of on and off. Ask the children to do such things as the following: "Step on the rug; Step off the rug; Put the crayons on the table; Take the crayons off the table." Continue with directions such as these: "Turn the water on; Turn the water off; Turn the TV on; Turn the TV off." If desired, let the children practice using the words "on" and "off" by giving directions to one another.

O Chains

Cut construction paper into 1- by 10-inch strips. Place the strips in a box and set out glue. Let the children use the paper strips to make chains of O's. If desired, hook the chains together as they are completed and hang them around the room.

O Is for Office

Create a pretend office in the corner of your room, using small tables for desks. Set out such things as pads of paper, play telephones, junk mail, pencils, paper clips, rubber stamps and ink pads. Let the children have fun playing in the office during your O unit.

The Letter O

Obstacle Course

Set up a simple obstacle course in your room. For example, include cardboard cartons to crawl through, small pillows to jump over, a long board to walk across and a padded footstool to climb over. Let the children take turns going through the obstacle course at various times throughout your O unit. On the final day make ribbons from construction paper and print O's on them. Present one ribbon to each child as he or she completes the obstacle course.

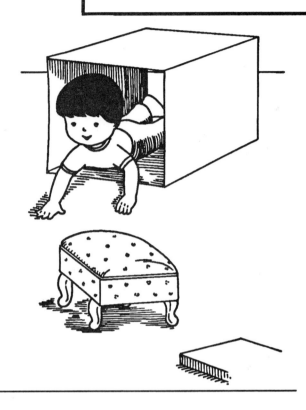

More Ideas for Fun With O

- Have an Orange Day.
- Make collages with paper ovals.
- Listen to recordings of opera or orchestra music.
- Form O's with fingers.
- Paint an ocean mural and attach octopus and oyster shapes.
- Pretend to be owls.
- Bake pretend foods in a toy oven.
- Glue pictures of O items on a giant O shape.

Let's Sing for the Letter O

Sung to: "Skip to My Lou"

Let's sing now for the letter O,
Let's sing some O words that we know.
Olive, owl and *octopus* too.
Oh, letter O, we do like you!

Repeat, substituting other words that begin with O for the words "olive," "owl" and "octopus."

Elizabeth McKinnon

O Snacks

Let the children help make omelets for snacktime. Serve with orange segments. Or make oatmeal and serve with orange juice.

Variation: Let the children make edible necklaces by threading O-shaped dry cereal on pieces of string.

Children's Books

- *Arthur's Eyes*, Marc Brown, (Little Brown).
- *Big Orange Splot*, Daniel Pinkwater, (Scholastic).
- *Herman the Helper*, Robert Kraus, (Simon and Schuster).
- *How to Hide an Octopus*, Ruth Heller, (Putnam).
- *Orchestranimals*, Fan Cameron, (Scholastic).
- *Spectacles*, Ellen Raskin, (Macmillan).

The Letter O

The Octopus
Sung to: "Little White Duck"

There are eight tentacles
Swimming in the ocean,
Eight tentacles making a commotion.
Who could belong to so many feet?
The octopus does and they help
    him eat.
He has eight tentacles
Swimming in the ocean,
Swim, swim, swim.

Judy Hall

Optometrist Song
Sung to: "Down by the Station"

Down at my office,
When you come to visit,
I have a big machine
To look into your eyes.
I can help you see more
If you're having trouble.
Click, click, click, click,
Look inside.

Jean Warren

Contributors:

Betty Ruth Baker, Waco, TX
Judy Hall, Wytheville, VA
Betty Silkunas, Lansdale, PA

Alphabet Patterns

Use the patterns on the following pages to make stick puppets, learning games, alphabet books and other teaching aids.

octopus

optometrist

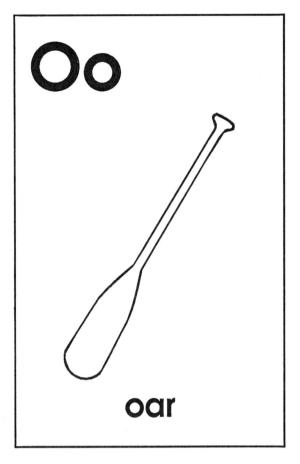

Oo

oar

Oo

octopus

Oo

onion

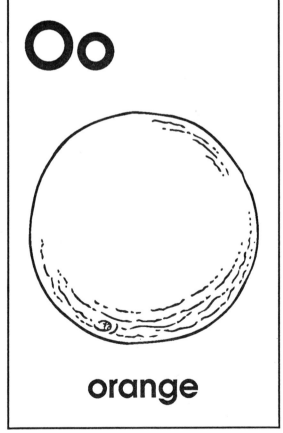

Oo

orange

© Warren Publishing House, Inc. 1991

Oo

ostrich

Oo

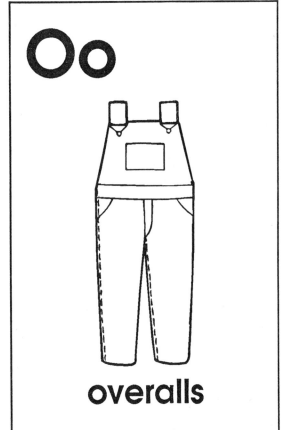

overalls

Oo

owl

Oo

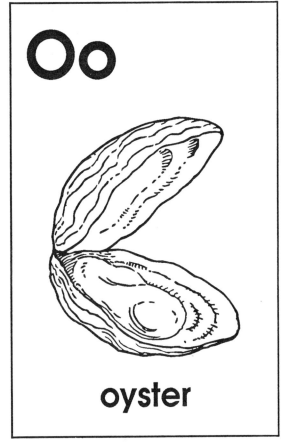

oyster

The Letter P

Display/Play Box for *P*

Decorate a box with the letter *P* to use throughout your *P* unit. Inside the box place items (or pictures of items) whose names begin with *P*. Below are some suggestions.

- pail
- paintbrush
- pajamas
- pan
- pancake
- paper
- parachute
- parrot
- paste
- peanut butter
- peanuts
- pear
- pen
- pencil
- penny
- pie pan
- pig
- pillow
- pine cone
- pizza
- placemat
- plate
- pocket
- popcorn
- postcard
- potato
- pumpkin
- puppet
- puppy

Popcorn *P*'s

Cut large letter *P* shapes out of heavy paper. Set out bowls of popped popcorn and shallow containers of glue. Let the children dip pieces of popcorn into the glue and then place them all over their letter shapes.

Variation: Let the children make purple fingerpaint designs on sheets of white paper. When dry, cut the papers into *P* shapes and display them around the room.

P Pancakes in the Pan

Print the letter *P* on an index card and tape it to the side of a large frying pan. Cut 2 ½-inch circles out of heavy brown cardboard for pancakes. Print *P*'s on most of the pancakes and print other letters on the rest. Spread out the pancakes around the frying pan. Then let the children take turns selecting *P* pancakes and transferring them to the pan with a pancake turner.

Variation: Place one pancake marked with *P* and two pancakes marked with other letters in the pan. Give the pancake turner to one child and have the child use it to transfer the *P* pancake to a plate. Continue in the same manner until everyone has had a turn.

Potato Printing

Make paint pads by placing folded paper towels in shallow containers and pouring on purple or pink tempera paint. Cut potatoes into chunks of various sizes. Let the children dip the potato chunks into the paint and then press them on pieces of construction paper to make prints.

Extension: If desired, turn the children's decorated papers into placemats by covering them with clear self-stick paper.

The Letter P

Paula Had a Party

Paula had a party, and I think you'll agree
That a lot of attention was paid to P.

Poodles and polar bears paraded by.
Pigeons and parakeets came to fly.

Penguins splashed around in Paula's pool.
People drank purple juice just to keep cool.

Peaches and pears were served on plates.
The peanuts and popcorn tasted just great.

Panda played the piano, ever so proud,
Till Paula shouted, "You're playing too loud!"

Then Paula looked around, her place was a mess.
She was tired of P, she needed a rest.

"Please leave my party!" Paula said.
Then Paula turned around and went to bed.

Susan M. Paprocki

Paper Plate Collages

Give each child a paper plate with the letter *P* printed on it. Let the children tear different kinds of paper into small pieces. Then have them glue the paper pieces around the letters on their plates.

Variation: Let the children glue magazine pictures of things whose names begin with *P* on their paper plates.

P's in the Pillowcase

Label a pillowcase with the letter P. Have the children sit on the floor in a circle. Place the pillowcase in the middle of the circle, along with objects from your P Display/Play Box (see page 156). Let each child in turn choose an object, name it and place it in the pillowcase. Then have the children take turns reaching inside the pillowcase and identifying the objects by touch.

Variation: Instead of using a pillowcase, decorate a box with a lid to look like a present (keep the lid free). After naming several objects with the group, hide one of the objects inside the box and let the children try guessing what's inside the present.

Pig Puzzles

Cut several identical pig shapes out of pink index cards or pink posterboard. Cut each pig shape into two puzzle pieces. Print an upper-case P on the left-hand piece and a lower-case P on the right-hand piece. Mix up all the puzzle pieces and place them in a pile. Then let the children take turns putting the pig puzzles together.

The Letter P

Puppet Parade

Cut out pictures of animals whose names begin with the letter *P*. Include any of the following: a puppy, a pig, a pony, a panda, a porcupine, a porpoise, a parrot, a penguin, a peacock or a parakeet. Mount the pictures on construction paper, trim around the edges and attach them to Popsicle sticks to make puppets. Hand out the puppets to the children and talk about the movements that the different animals make. Then play music and let the children act out the movements of their animal puppets as they parade around the room.

Playdough *P*'s

Set out balls of playdough, along with pieces of construction paper with large upper-case *P*'s printed on them. Let the children roll the playdough balls into snakes. Then have them place the snakes on top of the printed letters to form playdough *P*'s.

Extension: Let the children also make playdough objects whose names begin with *P*, such as pies, pancakes, pumpkins or pretzels.

P Picnic

Let the children help pack a picnic lunch made up of foods whose names begin with the letter *P*. For example, include any of the following: peanut butter sandwiches, pizza, pretzels, popcorn, pickles, pineapple, peaches or pears. Let the children enjoy their picnic outdoors or on a blanket spread out on the floor in your room.

Variation: Make pretzel *P*'s (see recipe on page 237).

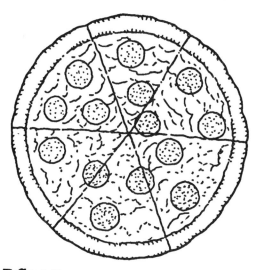

P Song
Sung to: "Bingo"

I know a word that starts with P,
And *pizza* is its name.
P-I-Z-Z-A, P-I-Z-Z-A, P-I-Z-Z-A,
And *pizza* is its name.

Repeat, each time substituting one of the following words for the word "pizza": "puppy, penny, panda, paper, piano, paint, peach, plate, purse."

Elizabeth McKinnon

More Ideas for Fun With *P*

- Play Peek-A-Boo.
- Recite "Peter Piper picked a peck of pickled peppers."
- Pretend to be popcorn popping in the pan.
- Practice pouring with a small pitcher.
- Pretend to play the piano.
- Count the number of pennies inside a purse.
- Match pairs of identical picture postcards.
- Weigh and compare a pound of potatoes and a pound of peanuts.
- Form *P*'s with pipe cleaners.

Children's Books:

- *Big Book of Mr. Small*, Lois Lenski, (Outlet).
- *I Can Be a Police Officer*, Catherine Matthias, (Children's Press).
- *Peanut Butter & Jelly*, Nadine Wescott, (Dutton).
- *Pig's Wedding*, Helme Heine, (Macmillan).
- *Possum Magic*, Mem Fox, (Abingdon).
- *Sloppy Kisses*, Elizabeth Winthrop, (Macmillan).

The Letter P

The Pig
Sung to: "Camptown Races"

The pig rolls in the mud all day,
Oink-oink, oink-oink.
That is what he likes to say,
Oink-oink-oink-oink-oink.
Curly tail that grows,
Pudgy little nose.
Mud is where he likes to be,
And it really shows.

Judy Hall

I'm a Police Officer
Sung to: "The Muffin Man"

You can trust a police officer,
Police officer, police officer.
You can trust a police officer,
If you need some help.

I will keep you safe from harm,
Safe from harm, safe from harm.
I will keep you safe from harm.
I'm a police officer.

Jean Warren

Contributors:

Rita Galloway, Harlingen, TX
Judy Hall, Wytheville, VA
Neoma Kreuter, Ontario, CA
Nancy C. Windes, Denver, CO

Alphabet Patterns

Use the patterns on the following pages to make stick puppets, learning games, alphabet books and other teaching aids.

pig

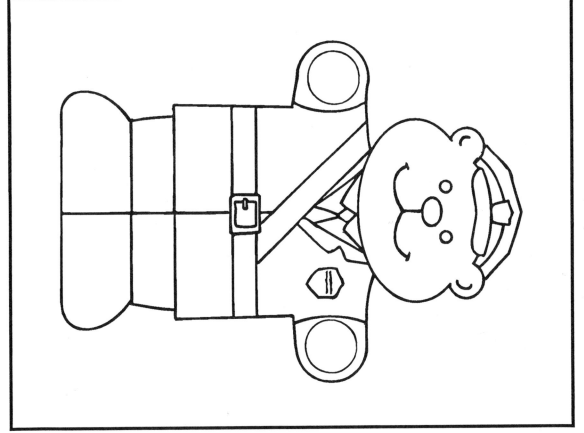

police officer

Pp

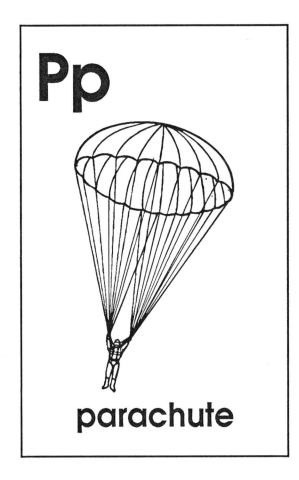

parachute

Pp

parrot

Pp

peacock

Pp

peanut

Pp

penguin

Pp

pig

Pp

pineapple

Pp

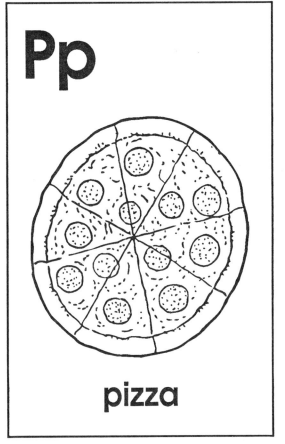

pizza

The Letter Q

Display/Play Box for Q

Decorate a box with the letter Q to use throughout your Q unit. Inside the box place items (or pictures of items) whose names begin with Q. Below are some suggestions.

- quail
- Quaker Oats box
- quarter
- queen
- question mark
- quill
- quilt
- Q-tips

Quarter Q's

Cut large letter Q shapes out of heavy paper. Make rubbings of quarters on white paper, using the side of a pencil point or a crayon. (If desired, let the children make their own quarter rubbings as a separate activity.) Cut out the rubbings and let the children glue the "quarters" on their letter Q shapes.

Variation: Let the children glue Q-tips on their letters. Or have them glue on large question marks cut from newspaper headlines and magazine ads.

Q Is for Quilt

Give each child a 9-inch square of construction paper that has been creased diagonally both ways. Set out diamond shapes cut from aluminum foil and colorful paper scraps. Let the children glue the diamond shapes on their squares in patterns, using the creases on their squares as guidelines. Arrange the squares in a rectangular shape on the floor and tape them all together to make a quilt. Display the quilt on a wall or a bulletin board, along with the title "Q is for Quilt."

Variation: Give each child a 9-inch square of construction paper that has been divided into nine squares. Let the children glue 3-inch squares of fabric in the squares on their papers to create quilt patterns. If desired, tape the children's papers together to make a group quilt.

Mother and Baby Quails

Choose one child to be the Mother Quail and let the other children be Baby Quails. Have the Mother Quail start walking around the room. Then sing the song below, each time signaling one of the Baby Quails to get in line behind the mother. Continue singing until everyone is in line. If desired, choose a new Mother Quail and start the game again.

Sung to: "Down by the Station"

Out in the forest
Early in the morning,
See the little Mother Quail
Walking to and fro.
See a little Baby Quail
Get in line behind her.
Quickly, quickly, off they go.

Elizabeth McKinnon

The Letter Q

Quill Pens

Explain to the children that people long ago wrote with quill pens, which they made from feathers. They sharpened the ends of the feathers into points and then dipped them in ink. Print Q's on pieces of construction paper and set out long feathers. Let the children hold the feathers like quill pens, pretend to dip them in ink and then practice tracing over the printed Q's.

Extension: Have the children dip the ends of their feathers into diluted food coloring "ink." Let them trace over the Q's on their papers or just draw designs.

Quacking for Q

Print Q's on five or six index cards and print other letters on several more cards. Have the children sit on the floor in front of you. Hold up the cards one at a time. Whenever the children see the letter Q, have them quack.

I Like Q
Sung to: "Twinkle, Twinkle, Little Star"

Q is for queen with a crown on her head,
Q is for quilt that covers my bed.
Q is for questions I like asking,
Q is for ducklings' quack-quack-quacking.
Q is for quarter and quick and quill,
I like Q and I always will.

Elizabeth McKinnon

More Ideas for Fun With Q

- Find the queens in a deck of playing cards.
- Quiver hands, arms, heads and whole bodies.
- Examine quarters with a magnifying glass.
- Quack specific numbers of times as number cards are flashed.
- Cut apples, oranges or round pie shapes into quarters.

Q Snacks

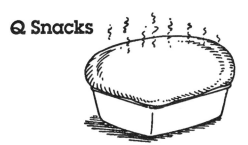

Use a favorite recipe to make quiche. Or let the children help make a quick bread such as the sugarless banana bread below.

Banana Bread — Heat ½ cup raisins in ¼ cup unsweetened frozen apple juice concentrate for 3 minutes over high heat. Pour the mixture into a blender container and puree. Add 1 egg, ¼ cup vegetable oil, 1 sliced banana and 1 teaspoon vanilla. Blend until smooth. In a large bowl mix together 1 cup whole-wheat flour, ½ teaspoon baking powder, ½ teaspoon baking soda, ¼ teaspoon salt and 2 teaspoons cinnamon. Stir in the ingredients from the blender container and add ½ cup chopped nuts, if desired. Pour the mixture into a greased loaf pan and bake at 350 degrees for 40 to 50 minutes.

Children's Books:

- *Patchwork Quilt*, Valerie Flournoy, (Dial).
- *Quail Song, A Pueblo Indian Folktale*, Valerie Carey, (Putnam).
- *Queen of Eene*, Jack Prelutsky, (Morrow).
- *Quicksand Book*, Tomie De Paola, (Holiday House).
- *The Quilt*, Ann Jonas, (Greenwillow).

The Letter Q

Little Quail
Sung to: "Frere Jacques"

Little quail, little quail,
Feathered head, feathered tail.
I like to watch you strutting by,
Or flapping as you start to fly.
Little quail, little quail.

Jean Warren

I'm a Busy Quilter
Sung to: "Eensy Weensy Spider"

I'm a busy quilter,
I sew and sew all day.
When my quilts are finished,
I can stop and play.
Sometimes my quilts are fancy,
Sometimes I make them plain.
Sometimes my quilts are different,
Sometimes they're all the same.

Jean Warren

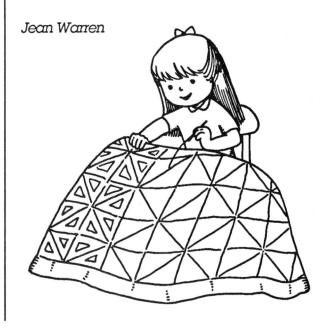

Contributors:

Betty Ruth Baker, Waco, TX
Rita Galloway, Harlingen, TX
Karen Kilimnik, Philadelphia, PA

Alphabet Patterns

Use the patterns on the following pages to make stick puppets, learning games, alphabet books and other teaching aids.

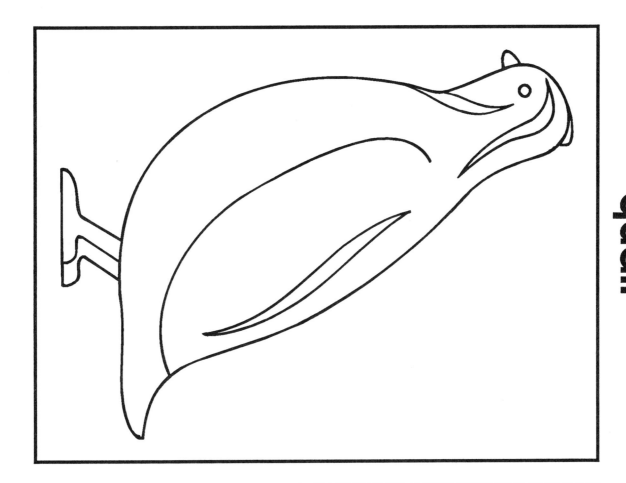

quail

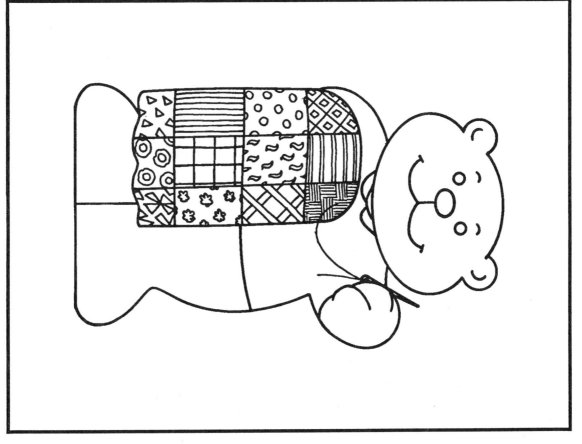

quilter

Qq
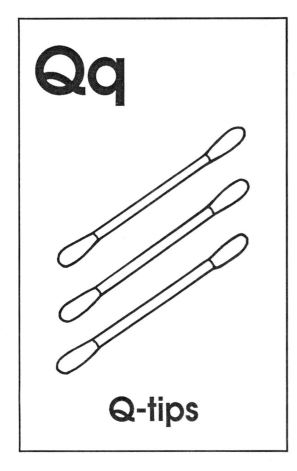
Q-tips

Qq

quail

Qq

quarter

Qq

queen

Qq

question mark

Qq

quiche

Qq

quill

Qq

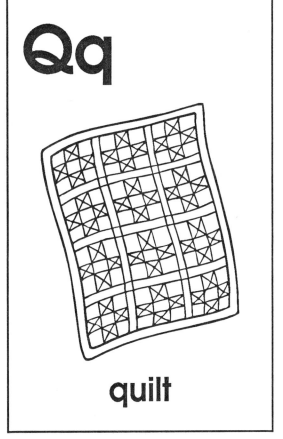

quilt

The Letter R

Display/Play Box for *R*

Decorate a box with the letter *R* to use throughout your *R* unit. Inside the box place items (or pictures of items) whose names begin with *R*. Below are some suggestions.

- rabbit
- radio
- raft
- rag
- rain coat
- rainbow
- raisins
- rake
- rattle
- reindeer
- ribbon

- ring
- robot
- rock
- rocket
- roller skates
- rolling pin
- rooster
- rope
- rug
- ruler

Ribbon *R*'s

Cut large letter *R* shapes out of heavy paper. Set out glue and different kinds of ribbon cut into short pieces. Let the children choose the ribbon pieces they want and glue them all over their letter shapes.

Variation: Let the children make red fingerpaint designs on sheets of white paper. When dry, cut the papers into large *R* shapes and display them around the room.

Robert the Robot

Make a robot by covering a box with aluminum foil, drawing on a face with permanent felt-tip markers and gluing on accordion-folded paper strips for arms. Print "Robert the Robot" on the box. In a bag place objects from your *R* Display/Play Box (see page 174). Explain to the children that Robert the Robot likes to collect things whose names begin with the letter *R*. Let each child have a turn reaching into the bag and removing an *R* object. Have the child name the object by saying, "Here is a _____ for Robert the Robot." Then have the child place the item in front of Robert.

Rickrack Rectangles

Give each child a small rectangle cut from construction paper. Set out pieces of rickrack. Let the children glue the rickrack pieces all over their rectangles. If desired, hang the rickrack rectangles from a coat hanger to make a mobile.

The Letter R

R Is for Raindrops

Cut a large umbrella shape out of colorful wrapping paper. Glue the shape on a piece of butcher paper and add a handle. Print "*R* is for Raindrops" at the top of the paper and then hang it on a wall at the children's eye level. Cut raindrop shapes out of light blue construction paper. Print *R*'s on most of the shapes and print other letters on the rest. Spread out the raindrops on a table. Let the children take turns selecting raindrops that have *R*'s printed on them and gluing them all around the umbrella on the butcher paper.

Rabbit Ears

For each child cut a headband and two rabbit ear shapes out of white construction paper. Print upper-case *R*'s on half of the ear shapes and lower-case *R*'s on the other half. Mix up the rabbit ears and spread them out on a table. Let each child in turn choose two ear shapes, one marked with an upper-case *R* and the other with a lower-case *R*. Have the children tape their rabbit ears to their headbands as shown in the illustration. Then tape together the ends of each child's headband and help the child put it on.

Remembering *R*

Cut a small letter *R* out of poster-board or heavy paper. Place two plastic bowls upside down on a table in front of the children. Put the posterboard *R* under one of the bowls. Slowly move the bowls around a few times. Then let the children take turns guessing under which bowl the *R* is hidden. When a child guesses correctly, say, "Good, (child's name) remembered where the *R* was." Let that child place the *R* under one of the bowls for the next round of the game. Continue until each child has made at least one correct guess.

Rock Matching Game

Collect five pairs of rocks ranging in size from small to large. Paint the rocks and allow them to dry. Group the rocks into pairs of matching sizes. Print an upper-case *R* on one of the rocks in each pair and a lower-case *R* on the other. Then mix up the rocks and let the children take turns finding the matching pairs.

Rice *R*'s

Tape a long piece of waxed paper to a tabletop. Use a permanent felt-tip marker to print a number of *R*'s on the waxed paper. Have the children use brushes to trace over the letters with a thick coating of white glue. Then let them sprinkle rice heavily all over the glue. Allow the letters to dry overnight. The next day, carefully lift the rice *R*'s off the waxed paper and hang them as mobiles.

The Letter R

Round Go the R's
Sung to: "Ten Little Indians"

Round and round and round go the R's,
Round and round and round go the R's,
Round and round and round go the R's,
Round and round the ring.

Round goes a rock and a rope and a ruler,
Round goes a rock and a rope and a ruler,
Round goes a rock and a rope and a ruler,
Round and round the ring.

Let three children at a time hold R items as
you sing and walk around in a circle.
Substitute the names of the items for the
words "rock," "rope" and "ruler."

Elizabeth McKinnon

More Ideas for Fun With R

- Have a Red Day.
- Recite favorite rhymes.
- Play records.
- Sing "Row, Row, Row Your Boat."
- Listen to the radio.
- Roll on the floor like rolling pins.
- Name rhyming words.
- Make finger rings out of colored pipe cleaners.
- Play rhythm instruments.
- Have fun with riddles.

Radish Relay

Have the children wear their rabbit ears from the activity on page 176 and line up in two rows. Give the first child in each row a radish shape cut from red construction paper. Have the two children hop like rabbits to a designated spot in the room. Then have them hop back and give the radishes to the next two children in line before taking their places at the ends of their rows. Continue in the same manner until each child has had a turn. If one row finishes before the other, have the children in that row sit down and cheer for those who are still taking their turns.

R Snacks

At snacktime serve rice, raisins or raspberries. Or let the children help make rainbow toast (see below).

Rainbow Toast — Pour small amounts of milk into bowls and add drops of different colored food coloring. Set out new paintbrushes. Help the children paint rainbows on slices of white bread with the colored milk. Then toast the bread slices and brush on melted butter, if desired.

Children's Books:

- *All Aboard ABC*, Doug Magee, (Dutton).
- *Hattie and the Fox*, Mem Fox, (Macmillan).
- *Railroad Book*, E. Boyd Smith, (Houghton Mifflin).
- *Rain*, Peter Spier, (Doubleday).
- *Rose in My Garden*, Arnold Lobel, (Scholastic).
- *Rosie's Walk*, Pat Hutchins, (Macmillan).

The Letter R

The Rooster
Sung to: "Pop! Goes the Weasel"

The rooster crows at the break of day,
To say the day is new.
We all know just what he'll say,
It's cock-a-doodle-doo!

Judy Hall

I'm a Railroad Engineer
Sung to: "Down by the Station"

Down at the station
Early in the morning,
See all the trains
Standing in a row.
I'm a railroad engineer,
I jump aboard my train.
Chug, chug, chug, chug,
Off I go.

Jean Warren

Contributors:
Betty Ruth Baker, Waco, TX
Rita Galloway, Harlingen, TX
Judy Hall, Wytheville, PA
Betty Silkunas, Lansdale, PA

Alphabet Patterns
Use the patterns on the following pages to make stick puppets, learning games, alphabet books and other teaching aids.

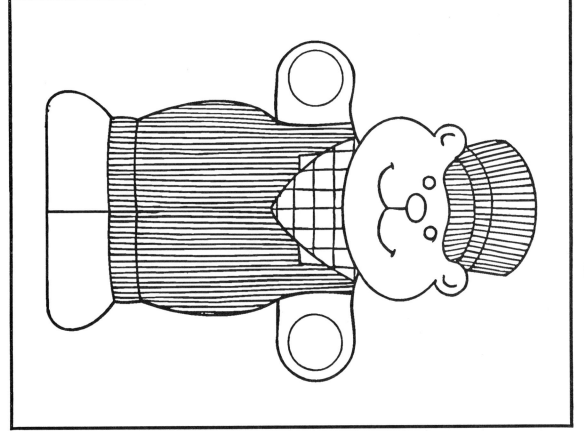

rooster

railroad engineer

The Letter *R*   181

Rr

raccoon

Rr

rainbow

Rr

rake

Rr

rhinoceros

Rr

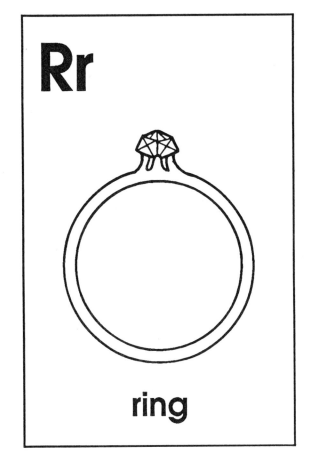

ring

Rr

robot

Rr

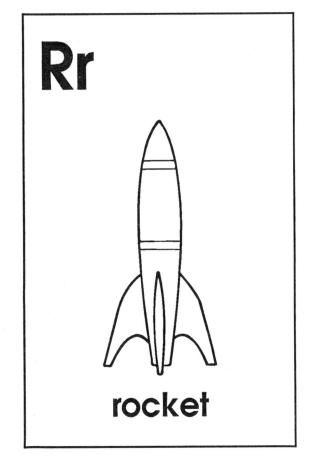

rocket

Rr

rooster

The Letter S

Display/Play Box for S

Decorate a box with the letter S to use throughout your S unit. Inside the box place items (or pictures of items) whose names begin with S. Below are some suggestions.

- sack
- sailboat
- sand
- sandpaper
- scale
- scarf
- scissors
- seashell
- seeds
- shirt
- shoe
- sled
- snake
- soap
- sock
- spider
- sponge
- spoon
- stamps
- star
- string
- suitcase

Star S's

Cut large letter S shapes out of heavy paper. Let the children decorate their letters by attaching star stickers. Or cut small star shapes from aluminum foil and construction paper and have the children glue them on their letters.

Variation: Let the children glue string, sand, sequins or seeds on their S shapes.

Shining Suns

Collect Styrofoam packing pieces shaped like half-spheres and S's. Let each child glue a half-sphere on a piece of construction paper to represent the center of a sun. Then have the children glue S-shaped foam pieces all around their suns for rays.

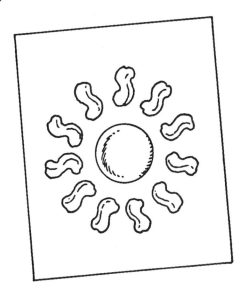

Sandy Snakes

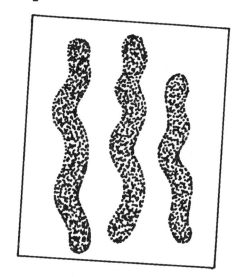

Let the children brush glue on sheets of paper to create long fat snakes. Have them sprinkle sand on the wet glue and then tap off the excess sand. When the glue has dried, encourage the children to feel their sandy snakes with their hands.

Super Sock Puppet

Use an old sock to create a Super Sock puppet. Stuff the toe and tie with yarn to make the puppet's head. Paint on a face or sew on features cut from felt. Then add a cape with the letter S printed on it. Use Super Sock throughout your S unit to do such things as saving or selecting items whose names start with S.

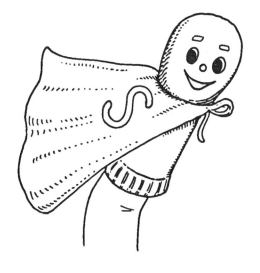

The Letter S

Secret in a Sock

Select several small objects from your *S* Display/Play Box (see page 184). Have the children sit on the floor in a circle. Secretly hide one of the objects inside a sock that has been labeled with the letter *S*. Then sing the song below and let the children take turns reaching inside the sock and trying to identify the object by touch. Follow the same procedure using the other *S* objects.

Sung to: "The Farmer in the Dell"

There's a secret in my sock,
A secret in my sock.
Can you guess, oh, can you guess
The secret in my sock?

Rita Galloway

S Stew

Collect canned or packaged food items whose names begin with *S*, such as spinach, spaghetti, squash, strawberries, syrup, sugar and salt. Label the items with the letter *S* and place them in a large grocery sack. Add several more food items whose names do not begin with *S* and that have been labeled with other letters. Set out a large pot and a wooden spoon. Print the letter *S* on a paper square and tape it to the side of the pot. Let the children take turns removing food items from the sack. If an item is not marked with *S*, have the child replace it and choose another one. If an item is marked with *S*, have the child name it, put it in the "stew pot" and give it a stir with the spoon. Continue playing the game until each child has had a chance to add a food item to the stew.

S Movement Game

Recite the poem below and have the children act out the movements described.

Stand in a circle, stoop down low,
Now stand up straight and tall.
Stamp, stamp, stamp your feet,
Now quietly curl up small.

Swing, swing, swing your arms,
Stretch, stretch your spines.
Sway, sway, swing and sway,
Now smile — you're looking fine!

Susan M. Paprocki

S's in the Sand

Place a layer of sand on a tray that has edges all around it. Print the letter *S* on an index card and tape it to the back edge of the tray. Let the children take turns drawing *S*'s in the sand with their fingers. Show them how to erase their letters by gently shaking the tray back and forth.

Variation: Use salt instead of sand. Or let the children use their fingers to draw *S*'s in shaving cream spread out over a flat surface.

Sponge *S*'s

Near a chalkboard place a bucket of water and several sponges. Let the children take turns dampening the sponges in the water and using them to draw large *S*'s on the dry chalkboard.

The Letter S

Silly *S* Song
Sung to: "Skip to My Lou"

I'll sing a silly *S* song for you,
I'll sing a silly *S* song for you.
A snake and a spoon went sailing in a shoe,
Sailing in a shoe by the seashore.

Repeat, substituting other words that begin
with *S* for the words "snake" and "spoon."

Elizabeth McKinnon

More Ideas for Fun With *S*

- Do sponge painting or spatter painting.
- Sing favorite songs.
- Snip paper strips into small pieces with scissors.
- Sort seeds, shells or socks.
- Trace over sandpaper *S*'s with fingers.
- Play on swings and slides.
- Run toy cars over *S*-curves drawn on butcher paper.
- Sniff and identify sweet scents.
- Sprout seeds.

S Snacks

Let the children help make spaghetti. Or read the folktale "Stone Soup" and follow up with the recipe below.

Stone Soup — Pour about 2 quarts water into a large pot and let the children put in a round smooth stone that has been scrubbed and boiled. Add chopped carrots, celery, potatoes, onions, zucchini and tomatoes. Bring to a boil and let simmer, covered, for about an hour. When the vegetables are tender, add instant broth or bouillon and season to taste. If desired, stir in small pieces of cooked meat or chicken shortly before serving.

Children's Books:

- *Sammy the Seal*, Syd Hoff, (Harper).
- *Sand Cake*, Frank Asch, (Putnam).
- *Seal Mother*, Mordicai Gersatein, (Dial).
- *Shoes from Grandpa*, Mem Fox, (Orchard).
- *Sing, Pierrot, Sing*, Tomie De Paola, (Harcourt).

The Letter S

I'm a Little Seal
Sung to: "The Farmer in the Dell"

I'm a little seal,
I'm lucky, I suppose.
I can catch a big round ball
Upon my little nose!

Sue Brown

I'm a Singer
Sung to: "Frere Jacques"

I'm a singer, I'm a singer,
Hear me sing, hear me sing.
I will sing your favorite song,
I can sing the whole day long.
Hear me sing, hear me sing.

Jean Warren

Contributors:

Betty Ruth Baker, Waco, TX
Jan Bodenstedt, Jackson, MI
Sue Brown, Louisville, KY
Rita Galloway, Harlingen, TX
Betty Silkunas, Lansdale, PA

Alphabet Patterns

Use the patterns on the following pages to make stick puppets, learning games, alphabet books and other teaching aids.

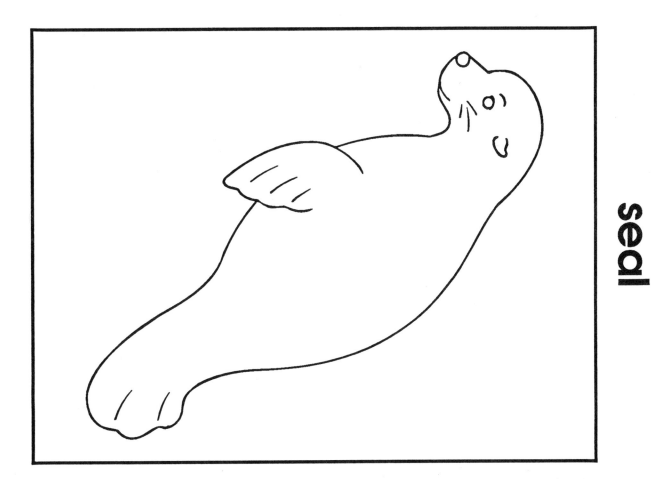

seal

singer

Ss

sailboat

Ss

sandwich

Ss

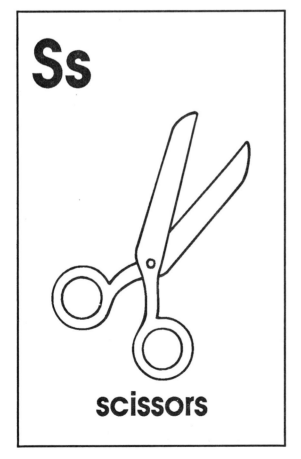

scissors

Ss

seal

Ss

sheep

Ss

shoes

Ss

skunk

Ss

star

Display/Play Box for *T*

Decorate a box with the letter *T* to use throughout your *T* unit. Inside the box place items (or pictures of items) whose names begin with *T*. Below are some suggestions.

- tablecloth
- tambourine
- tape
- teapot
- teddy bear
- telephone
- television
- tennis racket
- ticket
- tiger
- toothbrush
- top
- tractor
- train
- tray
- tree
- triangle
- tricycle
- truck
- T-shirt
- turtle

Toothpick *T*'s

Cut large letter *T* shapes out of heavy paper. Have the children brush glue on their letters. Then let them arrange wooden toothpicks on top of the glue.

Variation: Have the children glue dried tea leaves, tinsel or twigs on their *T* shapes. Or let them attach small pieces of colored plastic tape.

A Garden of Tulips

Place a piece of butcher paper on a table or on the floor. Using a green crayon or permanent felt-tip marker, print lower-case *T*'s on the butcher paper to represent flower stems with leaves. Cut tulip shapes out of different colors of construction paper. Let the children glue the tulip shapes on the tops of the lower-case *T*'s on the butcher paper to create a garden of tulips. When they have finished, display the paper on a wall or a bulletin board.

Tissue Triangle Art

Cut triangles out of different colors of tissue paper. Set out brushes and diluted glue. Give each child a piece of waxed paper. Have the children brush the glue on their papers and place the triangles on top of the glue. Encourage them to work on small areas at a time and to overlap their triangles to create new colors. For a shiny effect, brush more glue over the children's papers when they have finished. Attach construction paper frames. Then punch a hole in one corner of each frame and hang the papers from the ceiling.

The Letter T

Timer Game

Have the children sit in a circle. In the middle place several items from your *T* Display/Play Box (see page 194). Name each of the items with the group. Have the children close their eyes while you hide one of the items in a bag or a box. When they open their eyes, set a kitchen timer for the desired number of seconds and have the children try to guess which item you have hidden before the timer rings. Let the first child to guess correctly hide an item for the next round of the game. Or have the child choose someone who has not yet had a turn. Continue until every child has had a chance to hide a *T* item.

Tongue Depressor Games

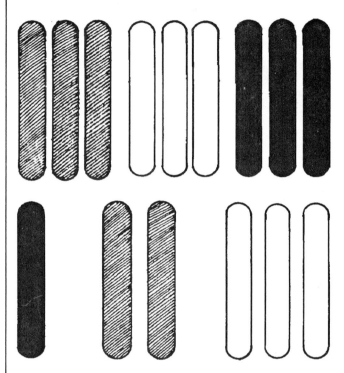

Color sets of tongue depressors with red, yellow and blue felt-tip markers. Let the children use the tongue depressors for counting and sorting games. Or draw vertical red, yellow and blue lines in color patterns on index cards. Have the children use the cards as guides to create color patterns with the tongue depressors.

Extension: Let the children use the tongue depressors to form *T*'s, triangles or other simple shapes.

Variation: Use colored plastic toothpicks instead of tongue depressors.

Train Ticket Game

Give each child two construction paper tickets, one marked with *T* and the other marked with another letter. Line up chairs to form a train and choose one child to be the Conductor. As the other children step forward to board the train, have the Conductor collect a *T* ticket from each one. Let the children enjoy a short "train ride." When the ride is over, redistribute the tickets, choose a new Conductor and start the game again. Continue playing until each child has had a turn being the Conductor.

Signing for *T*

Print *T*'s on five or six index cards and print other letters on several more cards. Have the children sit on the floor in front of you. Show them how to use their pointer fingers to form the letter *T*. Then hold up the cards one at a time. Whenever the children see the letter *T*, have them make the *T* sign with their fingers.

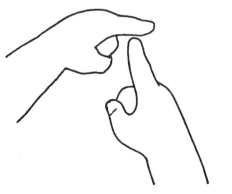

T Bags in the Teapot

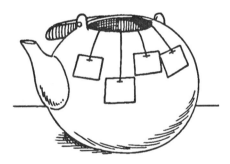

Save the tags and strings from used tea bags. On the ends of the strings, attach small pictures of things whose names begin with *T*. Place the pictures in a teapot with the strings and tags hanging out around the top. Then let each child have a turn taking out a "*T* bag" and naming the picture.

The Letter T

Teddy Bear, Teddy Bear

Have the children pretend to be teddy bears. As you recite the poem below, let them act out the movements described.

Teddy Bear, Teddy Bear, turn around,
Teddy Bear, Teddy Bear, touch the ground.
Teddy Bear, Teddy Bear, stand tall now.
Teddy Bear, Teddy Bear, take a bow.
Teddy Bear, Teddy Bear, touch your nose.
Teddy Bear, Teddy Bear, tap your toes.

Adapted Traditional

More Ideas for Fun With *T*

- Talk on a toy telephone.
- Form *T*'s on the floor with bodies.
- Paint with toothbrushes.
- Stencil *T*'s on T-shirts.
- Cover *T*'s with textured materials for touching.
- Play on a teeter-totter.
- Make a terrarium.
- Tell tall tales and record them on tape.
- Talk about favorite TV programs.
- Walk on tiptoe.

Tap Your Toe for *T*
Sung to: "Row, Row, Row Your Boat"

Tap, tap, tap your toe,
Tap your toe for *T*.
Tap for train and turkey and toy,
Tap, tap, one, two, three.

Repeat, substituting other words that begin with *T* for the words "train," "turkey" and "toy."

Elizabeth McKinnon

T Party

Let the children enjoy a "*T* party" at snacktime. Serve tuna finger sandwiches or buttered toast triangles and tomato wedges. Set out teacups and a small teapot filled with warm tea. Let the children take turns pouring the tea into their teacups.

Variation: Fill the teapot with tomato juice instead of tea.

Children's Books:

- *Franklin in the Dark*, Paulette Bourgrois, (Scholastic).
- *I Wish I Could Fly*, Ron Maris, (Greenwillow).
- *My Teacher Sleeps in School*, Leatie Weiss, (Viking).
- *Tikki Tikki Tembo*, Arlene Mosel, (Holt).
- *Tingalayo*, Raffi, (Crown).
- *What If the Teacher Calls on Me?*, Alan Gross, (Children's Press).

The Letter T

I'm a Teacher
Sung to: "Twinkle, Twinkle, Little Star"

A, B, C, D, E, F, G,
I'm a teacher, can't you see?
I plan lessons every day,
I help children work and play.
A, B, C, D, E, F, G,
I'm a teacher, can't you see?

Jean Warren

The Turtle
Sung to: "Pop! Goes the Weasel"

The turtle wears a shell on his back,
He walks so very slow.
Just put him in the water and watch.
He can really go!

Judy Hall

Contributors:

Jan Bodenstedt, Jackson, MI
Rita Galloway, Harlingen, TX
Judy Hall, Wytheville, VA
Susan Peters, Upland, CA

Alphabet Patterns

Use the patterns on the following pages to make stick puppets, learning games, alphabet books and other teaching aids.

turtle

teacher

Tt

tambourine

Tt

telephone

Tt

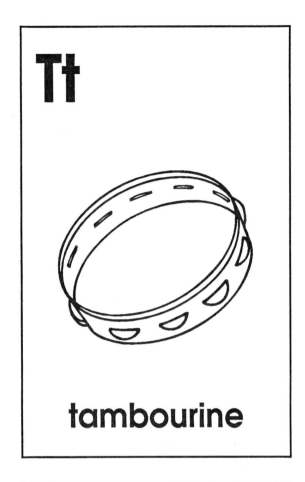

tiger

Tt

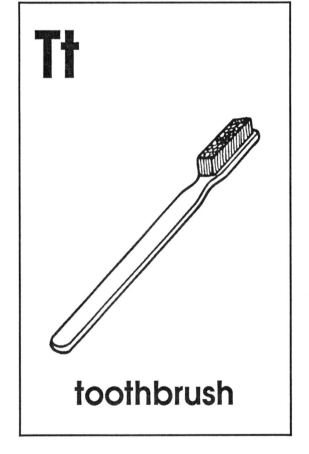

toothbrush

Tt

train

Tt

tree

Tt

tricycle

Tt

turtle

The Letter U

Display/Play Box for *U*

Decorate a box with the letter *U* to use throughout your *U* unit. Inside the box place items (or pictures of items) whose names begin with *U*. Below are some suggestions.

- ukulele
- umbrella
- umpire
- underwear
- unicorn
- unicycle
- uniform

"*U*" *U*'s

Cut large letter *U* shapes out of heavy paper. Make small "*U*'s" by cutting the top parts off of self-stick reinforcement circles (available at stationery stores). Let the children stick the small *U*'s all over their letter shapes.

Uniform Collage

Place a piece of butcher paper on a table or on the floor. Print the letter *U* at the top of the paper. Set out pictures of people dressed in different kinds of uniforms. For example, you might include police officers, fire fighters, mail carriers, doctors, gas station attendants, food service people and baseball or football players. Let the children select pictures and glue them on the butcher paper to create a uniform collage. Display the collage on a wall or a bulletin board and talk about the different uniforms with the children.

U Mobile

Hang a small umbrella upside down. Cut out pictures of things whose names begin with *U*. Mount the pictures on plain paper. Print the letter *U* on the back of each picture. Then hang the pictures from the upside-down umbrella to create a mobile. Let the children take turns naming the pictures.

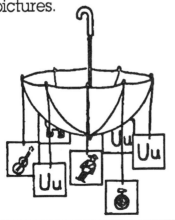

Thumbs Up for *U*

Print *U*'s on five or six index cards and print other letters on several more cards. Have the children sit in front of you. Then hold up the cards, one at a time, and have the children make the "thumbs-up" sign whenever they see the letter *U*.

The Letter U

U Is for Under

Cut *U* shapes out of construction paper. Place the *U*'s under objects around the room, such as chairs, tables, books and toys. Let the children walk around and look under different objects to find the *U*'s. (Make sure each child finds at least one.) When all the *U*'s have been found, give directions such as these: "Place a *U* under the teddy bear; Place a *U* under the basket; Place a *U* under the wagon."

Un-Activities

Have the children sit with you in a circle. Let them try doing "un-activities" such as the following: untie a shoe, unbutton a button, unzip a zipper, unbend a finger, unfold a piece of paper, uncover a box, unwrap a package. Follow up by letting the children load and unload a toy truck.

U Map Fun

Draw a straight road on a long piece of butcher paper taped to the floor. Cut arches out of the wide sides of a shoebox and print the word "underpass" above each arch. Place the box over the road and tape it to the butcher paper. At each end of the road, draw a U-turn arrow and a "U-turn" sign beside it. Let the children take turns driving toy cars on the road, passing under the underpass and making U-turns at the road ends.

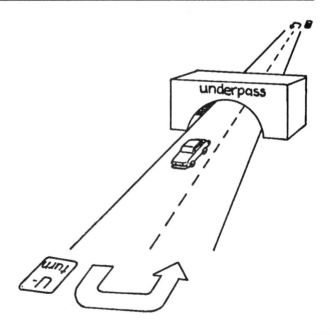

Umbrella Color Game

Cut one umbrella shape each from the following colors of felt: green, red, purple, blue, yellow, orange. As you read the poem below, let the children help place the appropriate colored umbrellas on a flannelboard.

We keep our umbrellas, so perky and gay,
Ready and waiting for a rainy day.

Here is a green one to keep me dry
When I open it up and hold it high.

Have you seen the umbrella that's ruby red?
It looks so regal held over my head.

The rain can get heavy, oh me, oh my,
But the purple umbrella will keep me dry.

I love the umbrella of sweet sky blue.
It's big enough for both me and you.

The yellow umbrella is bright like the sun.
Jumping puddles with it is ever so fun.

The orange umbrella is saved for showers,
The kind of rain that wakes up the flowers.

Our umbrellas are fun and so nice to see.
Just look at them all, I'm sure you'll agree.

Susan M. Paprocki

The Letter U

My Umbrella

Recite the poem below and let the children act out the movements.

My umbrella goes up
    (Raise arms high, fingers touching.)
And I go under,
Whenever I hear
The sound of thunder.

It is wild and windy,
    (Move raised arms back and forth.)
See the weather vane.
My umbrella is pulling
With the blowing rain.

Now it is still
    (Hold raised arms in place.)
And I see the sun.
Down comes my umbrella,
    (Lower arms to sides.)
Time now for fun!

Susan M. Paprocki

U Song

Sung to: "My Bonnie Lies Over the Ocean"

Let's stand up and sing for umbrella,
Umbrella starts with U.
Let's stand up and sing for umbrella
And for the letter U.
U, U, U, U,
Let's sing for the letter U, U, U.
U, U, U, U,
Let's sing for the letter U.

Repeat, substituting other words that begin with U for the word "umbrella."

Elizabeth McKinnon

More Ideas for Fun With *U*

- Throw a ball underhand.
- Pretend to be ushers and show people to their seats.
- Make a mural showing undersea life.
- Walk upstairs.
- Bring in photos of uncles to share and discuss.
- Listen to the story of the Ugly Duckling.
- Take turns strumming a ukulele.
- Bend pipe cleaner segments into *U* shapes.

Upside-Down Sundaes

Talk with the children about how sundaes are usually made. Then give them each a clear plastic cup and let them have fun making "upside-down sundaes." Have them first sprinkle chopped nuts or dry cereal in the bottoms of their cups. Next, have them add some strawberry syrup (see recipe below). Finally, let them spoon in small amounts of plain yogurt. Before the children eat their sundaes, encourage them to stir all the ingredients together.

Strawberry Syrup — Place 1 cup strawberries and ¼ cup unsweetened frozen apple juice concentrate in a blender container. Process until smooth.

Children's Books:

- *Ronald Morgan Goes to Bat,* Patricia Giff, (Viking).
- *Sarah's Unicorn,* Bruce and Katherine Coville, (Harper).
- *Teammates,* Peter Golenbock, (Harcourt).
- *Ugly Duckling,* Marianna Mayer, (Macmillan).
- *Umbrella,* Taro Yashima, (Viking).
- *Unicorn and the Lake,* Marianna Mayer, (Dial).

The Letter U

Unicorn Song
Sung to: "Pop! Goes the Weasel"

One night I dreamed of a little
   white horse
That had a great big horn
Right in the middle of its head.
It was a unicorn.
I rode all night upon its back,
As I dreamed along.
But when the morning light
   appeared,
Poof! It was gone.

Jean Warren

Explain to the children that a unicorn is an
imaginary animal.

I'm the Umpire
Sung to: "Take Me Out to the Ball Game"

I like to work at the ball games,
I like to work with a crowd.
I judge the balls and the pop-up flies,
I rule what's right and I'll tell you why.
I'm the ump-ump-ump-ump-ump-umpire,
And every game is the same.
'Cause it's one, two, three strikes
   you're out
At the old ball game!

Jean Warren

Contributors:
Jan Bodenstedt, Jackson, MI

Alphabet Patterns
Use the patterns on the following
pages to make stick puppets, learning games, alphabet books and
other teaching aids.

unicorn

umpire

The Letter *U*   **211**

Uu

ukelele

Uu

umbrella

Uu

umpire

Uu

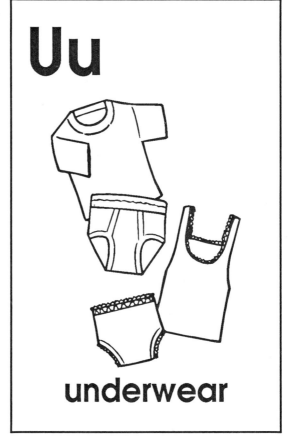

underwear

Uu

unicorn

Uu

unicycle

Uu

uniform

The Letter V

Display/Play Box for *V*

Decorate a box with the letter *V* to use throughout your *V* unit. Inside the box place items (or pictures of items) whose names begin with *V*. Below are some suggestions.

- vacuum cleaner
- valentine
- van
- vase
- Velcro
- velvet
- vest
- vine
- vinegar
- violets
- violin
- volleyball

Velvet *V*'s

Cut large letter *V* shapes out of heavy paper. Cut velvet (or any kind of velvet-like material) into small pieces. Let the children glue the velvet pieces all over their letter shapes.

V Flowers in the Vase

Label a vase with the letter *V*. Cut flower shapes out of construction paper. Print *V*'s on most of the shapes and print other letters on the rest. Attach straws or Popsicle sticks to the flower shapes for stems. Explain to the children that only the *V* flowers can be placed in the vase. Then let them take turns selecting a flower and deciding whether to put it into the vase or leave it out. Continue until all the *V* flowers are in the vase.

Tissue Paper Violets

For each child print the letter *V* at the top of a piece of white construction paper. Use a green crayon to draw short stems on each paper. Cut purple tissue paper into small squares and set out shallow containers of glue. Let the children twist the tissue squares around the eraser ends of pencils to create violets. Then have them dip the violets into the glue and place them on the tops of the stems on their papers. When the glue has dried, display the children's papers on a wall or a bulletin board.

The Letter V

Signing for *V*

Print *V*'s on five or six index cards and print other letters on several more cards. Have the children sit in front of you. Show them how to make the "*V* for victory" sign with their index and middle fingers. Then hold up the cards one at a time. Whenever the children see the letter *V*, have them make the "*V* for victory" sign.

V Formations

Have the children sit on the floor. Let them form *V*'s with their feet, their legs, their fingers, their hands and then with their upraised arms. Follow up by having the children choose partners and form *V*'s on the floor with their bodies.

Volcano Fun

Make a "volcano" by placing a small paper cup upright in a pie pan and forming a mountain around it with clay or playdough. Inside the cup place a tablespoon of baking soda. Let the children take turns adding tablespoons of vinegar to the cup and observing as the volcano "erupts."

Take a Vote

Let the children vote on such things as whether to play indoors or outdoors or whether to have orange juice or apple juice for a snack. Have them indicate their votes by raising their hands or standing up. Count the votes with the children and compare the total numbers. Be prepared to follow through on majority votes.

V Vests

Make a vest for each child by cutting a neck hole in the bottom of a large grocery bag and two armholes in the sides. Cut open the front of the bag from the bottom edge up to the neck hole. Print a large *V* on the back of each vest. Let the children trace over their *V*'s with glue and sprinkle on glitter. When the glue has dried, have the children use crayons or felt-tip markers to decorate the other parts of their vests. Help the children put on their vests and let them wear them throughout the day.

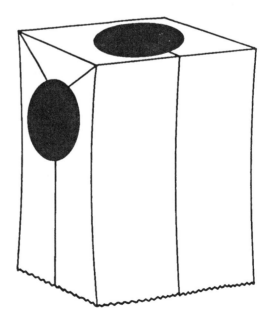

The Letter V

I Love to Make the Letter V
Sung to: "Pop! Goes the Weasel"

I love to make the letter V
For everyone to see.
> (Form V with two fingers.)

V is for vinegar, V is for van,
And V is for victory!

Repeat, substituting other words that begin
with V for the words "vinegar" and "van."

Elizabeth McKinnon

More Ideas for Fun With V

- Pretend to vacuum a carpet.
- Watch a videotape.
- Try on a hat with a visor.
- Talk about foods that contain lots of vitamins.
- Play "volleyball" with a balloon.
- Take a walk down a street to look for vans.
- Visit a veterinarian's office.
- Make valentine collages.
- Glue pictures of vegetables on a green yarn "vine."
- Talk about vacation fun.
- Form V's with straws, pencils or Popsicle sticks.

Sensory V's

Use the following activities to help the children explore the letter *V* with their five senses.

- Feel the texture of a velour shirt or other item of clothing.
- Sniff cotton balls scented with violet cologne, vanilla and vinegar.
- Taste an unfamiliar vegetable.
- Listen to violin music.
- Look through magazines to find pictures of things whose names begin with *V*.

Veggie Snacks

At snacktime let the children help prepare fresh vegetables for dipping. For example, you might wish to serve carrot and celery sticks, cucumber spears, zucchini slices, cherry tomatoes and cauliflower florets. Have the children arrange the vegetables on a large platter. Give them each a small plate with a spoonful of dip on it (see recipe below). Then let them help themselves to the vegetables.

Vegetable Dip — Stir together ¼ cup plain yogurt, ½ teaspoon lemon juice and ½ teaspoon dry Italian salad dressing mix.

Children's Books:

- *Eli*, Bill Peet, (Houghton Mifflin).
- *If You Were an Animal Doctor*, Ellen Levine, (Scholastic).
- *Moses the Kitten*, James Herriot, (St. Martin).
- *Petunia, I Love You*, Roger Duvoisin, (Knopf).
- *The Valentine Bears*, Eve Bunting, (Houghton Mifflin).
- *The Velveteen Rabbit*, Margery Williams, (Holt).

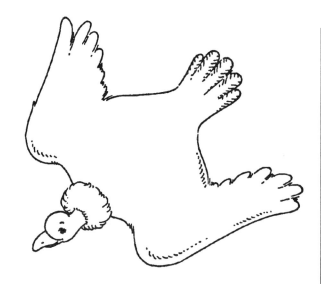

I'm a Great Big Vulture
Sung to: "I'm a Little Teapot"

I'm a great big vulture
In the sky,
Flying in a circle,
Oh, so high.
I just love to soar
Around and around.
Then down I swoop
Right to the ground.

Elizabeth McKinnon

I'm a Veterinarian
Sung to: "Oh, My Darling Clementine"

I'm a vet, I'm a vet,
I'm a veterinarian.
I take care of the animals,
And I treat them one by one.

I give shots, I set legs,
And sometimes I operate.
I take care of the animals,
'Cause I think they are just great.

Bring your dogs, bring your cats,
Bring your hamsters one by one.
I take care of the animals,
I'm a veterinarian.

Repeat, letting the children substitute other
animal names for the words "dogs," "cats"
and "hamsters."

Jean Warren

Contributors:
Ellen Javernick, Loveland, CO

Alphabet Patterns
Use the patterns on the following
pages to make stick puppets, learning games, alphabet books and
other teaching aids.

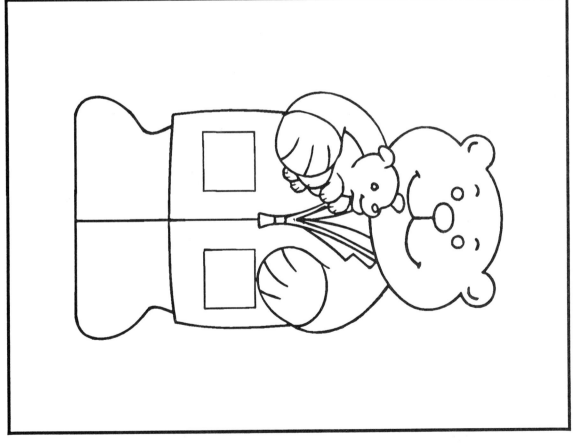

vulture

veterinarian

The Letter *V*   **221**

Vv

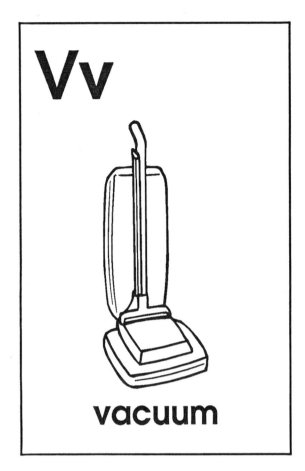

vacuum

Vv

valentine

Vv

van

Vv

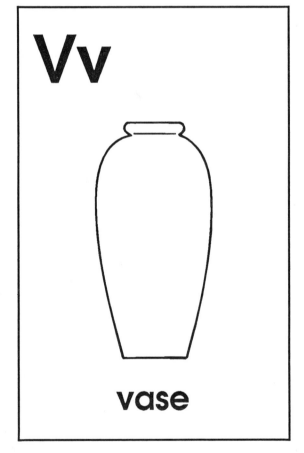

vase

Vv

vest

Vv

violets

Vv

violin

Vv

volleyball

The Letter W

Display/Play Box for W

Decorate a box with the letter W to use throughout your W unit. Inside the box place items (or pictures of items) whose names begin with W. Below are some suggestions.

- wagon
- wallet
- wallpaper
- walnut
- washcloth
- wastebasket
- watch
- watermelon
- waxed paper
- whale
- wheel
- whisk broom
- windmill
- window
- wishbone
- wood

Wallpaper W's

Cut large letter W shapes out of heavy paper. Set out glue and wallpaper samples. Let the children tear the wallpaper into small pieces and glue them all over their letters.

Variation: Have the children glue pasta wheels on their W shapes.

Wagon Fun

Label a wagon with the letter *W*. Beside it place items from your *W* Display/Play Box (see page 224). Have the children sit with you on the floor. Let them take turns choosing a *W* item, naming it and placing it in the wagon. Then remove the items from the wagon and put them in various places around the room. Let the children pull the wagon around to collect the items as you give such directions as these: "Find a washcloth to put in the wagon; Find a watch to put in the wagon; Find a walnut to put in the wagon."

Watch Collages

Give each child a piece of construction paper with the letter *W* printed on it. Have the children look through magazines and tear or cut out pictures of watches (or set out precut pictures). Let the children glue the pictures on their papers to create watch collages.

Extension: Make simple watches from construction paper that can be taped around the children's wrists. Print large *W*'s on the watch faces. Let the children wear their watches throughout the day.

The Letter W

W's in Wallets

Collect five or six wallets (or make wallets out of construction paper). Label each wallet with the letter W. Place a picture of something whose name begins with W inside each wallet. Then put the wallets in a basket. Let each child in turn take a wallet from the basket and name the letter on it. Then have the child open the wallet and name the picture inside. Have the child replace the wallet before the next child takes a turn. Continue until everyone has had a chance to choose a wallet and name a picture.

Waves of W's

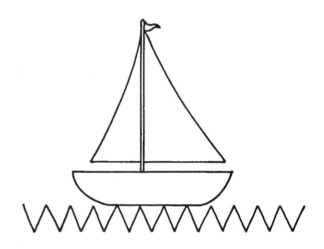

Draw a picture of a boat in the center of a piece of butcher paper. Underneath the boat draw continuous lines of W's for waves. Let the children trace over the W waves with blue crayons or felt-tip makers.

Variation: Let the children use chalk to trace over W waves drawn on a chalkboard.

Winking for W

Print W's on five or six index cards and print other letters on several more cards. Have the children sit in front of you. Then hold up the cards, one at a time, and have the children wink whenever they see the letter W.

Variation: Have the children wave instead of wink.

Willie Worm Puppets

Give each child a small paper cup with a finger-sized hole cut in the bottom. Let the children fill their cups partway with torn scraps of brown paper. Read the poem that follows. At the end of the poem, have the children stick their index fingers up through the holes in their cups and wiggle them like worms.

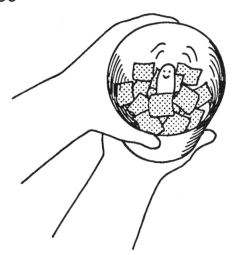

I have a pet named Willy
Who lives at home with me.
I keep him in this special cup
So all my friends can see.

Where, oh, where is Willy?
Oh, where can Willy be?
Come out now, little Willy,
So all my friends can see.

He is a little timid.
I must be very firm.
Come out now, little Willy!
Come out, my Willy Worm!

Jean Warren

Wood Fun

Set out scrap wood pieces, along with toys and other objects that are made from wood. Add several more objects that are made of plastic, metal or other materials. Have the children describe the textures, weights and any special features of the different objects. Then let them sort the objects into wood and non-wood piles.

The Letter W

W Walking

When it's time for the children to move from one area to another, have them walk in different "W ways" to get there. For example, ask them to waddle like ducks, wiggle along like worms or waltz like dancers. Or have them pretend to be walruses, wallabies, woodpeckers or whales as they walk.

More Ideas for Fun With W

- Name white objects in the room.
- Have a Wild West Day and wear western-style clothes.
- Toss crumpled paper into a wastepaper basket.
- Weave yarn around notched posterboard squares.
- Talk about the weather. Is it wet, windy or warm?
- Draw matching numbers of whiskers on numbered walrus faces.
- Talk in whispers.
- Learn about wheelchairs.
- Pretend to wash walls and windows.
- Make wishes.

Welcome, Little W

Sung to: "Twinkle, Twinkle, Little Star"

Welcome, little W,
We like you, we really do.
Waffles that we love to eat,
Watermelons, oh, so sweet.
W, we'll wave today,
When we see you come our way.

Welcome, little W,
We like you, we really do.
Worms and wagons here and there,
Walls and windows everywhere.
W, we'll wave today,
When we see you come our way.

Continue with similar verses, substituting other words that begin with W for the words "worms," "wagons," "walls" and "windows."

Elizabeth McKinnon

W Snacks

Let the children snack on watermelon or walnuts. Or cook pasta wheels and serve them with spaghetti sauce. If desired, use pieces of waxed paper for placemats and let the children take turns being waiters and waitresses.

Children Books:

- *Bert Dow: Deep-Water Man*, Robert McCloskey, (Viking).
- *I Can Be an Author*, Ray Broekel, (Childrens Press).
- *Stingbean's Trip to the Shining Sea*, Vera Williams, (Scholastic).
- *Whale in the Sky*, Anne Siberell, (Dutton).
- *Wilfrid Gordon McDonald Partridge*, Mem Fox, (Kane Miller).
- *Wolf's Chicken Stew*, Keiko Kasza, (Putnam).

The Letter W

I'm a Great Big Whale
Sung to: "I'm a Little Teapot"

I'm a great big whale,
Watch me swim.
Here is my blowhole,
Here are fins.
See me flip my tail as down I go,
Then up I come and "whoosh!" I blow.

Elizabeth McKinnon

I'm a Writer
Sung to: "Frere Jacques"

I'm a writer, I'm a writer,
I write stories, I write songs.
I can make you laugh or cry,
I can make you dream, that's why
I'm a writer, I'm a writer.

Jean Warren

Contributors:

Betty Ruth Baker, Waco, TX
Jan Bodenstedt, Jackson, MI
Rita Galloway, Harlingen, TX
Marilyn Dais Machosky,
    Westerville, OH
Susan Peters, Upland, CA

Alphabet Patterns

Use the patterns on the following pages to make stick puppets, learning games, alphabet books and other teaching aids.

whale

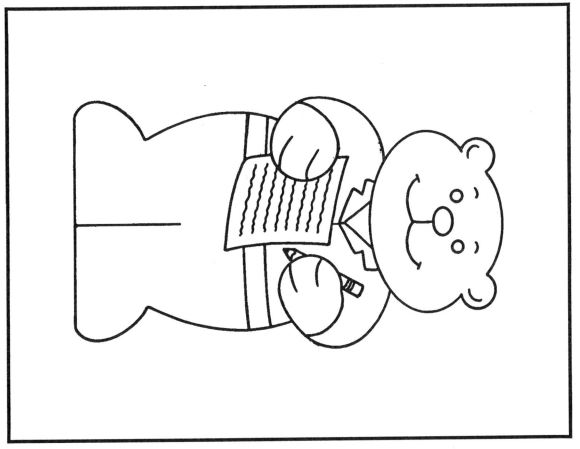

writer

Ww

wagon

Ww

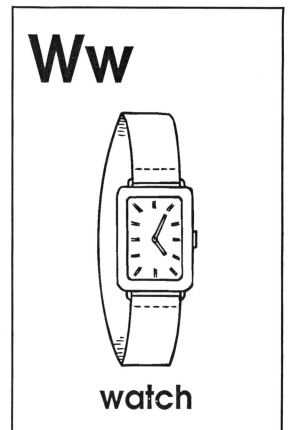

watch

Ww

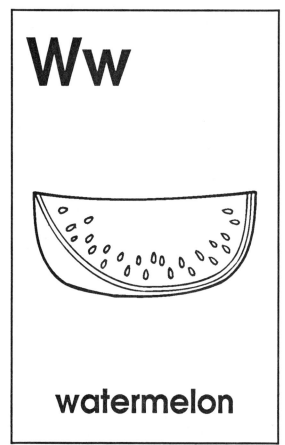

watermelon

Ww

whale

Ww

wheel

Ww

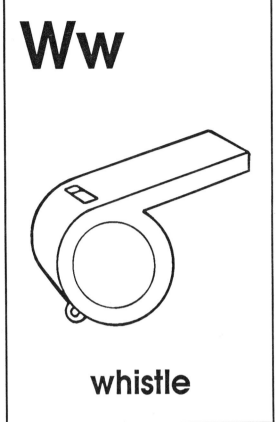

whistle

Ww

windmill

Ww

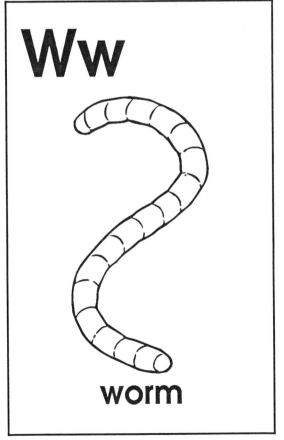

worm

The Letter X

Display/Play Box for *X*

Decorate a box with the letter *X* to use throughout your *X* unit. Inside the box place items (or pictures of items) whose names begin with *X*. Below are some suggestions.

- X-ray
- xylophone
- *X*'s (cut from cardboard)

"X" X's

Cut large letter *X* shapes out of heavy paper. Set out glue and small construction paper strips. Show the children how to glue the strips together to form *X*'s. Then let them glue their construction paper *X*'s on their large letter *X* shapes.

Variation: Have the children use strips of colored plastic tape to make *X*'s on their letter shapes.

X Marks the Spot

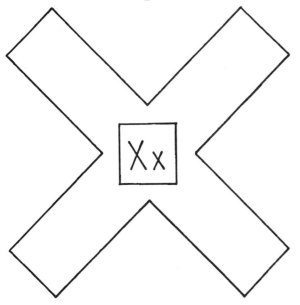

Tape a large posterboard X to the floor (or make an X with masking tape). Print X's and other letters on Post-it brand notes and stick them on objects around the room. Let the children walk around and search for the X notes. Whenever a child finds one, have him or her remove it and then stick it to the center of the large X on the floor. Continue until each child has found at least one X note.

Extension: Follow up by playing an "X Marks the Spot" game. Attach a squeaky toy to the center of the X on the floor. Then let the children take turns trying to toss a beanbag onto the center of the X to make the toy squeak.

Xylophone Game

Print large X's and other letters on separate pieces of construction paper and tape them to the floor in a circle. Set out a toy xylophone and demonstrate how it is played. Have the children walk around the circle. Whenever you play a note on the xylophone, have them stop. If they are standing on an X, have them cross their arms and hold them up. If desired, let the children take turns playing notes on the xylophone to stop the action. Continue the game as long as interest lasts.

Variation: Play tunes on the xylophone as the children walk around the circle. Have them stand in place whenever you stop playing.

The Letter X

X's Are for Kisses

Let the children make greeting cards to give to parents or special friends. Give each child a folded piece of construction paper with "I Love You" or "You Are Special" printed on the front. Let the children add decora-tions as desired. Inside each card print "X's are for kisses." Help each child sign his or her name. Then let the children print as many X "kisses" as they wish on the insides of their cards.

Exploring X-Rays

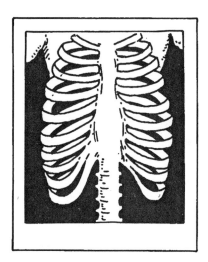

Check to see if a doctor, a dentist or a veterinarian can provide you with outdated or discarded X-rays. Hang the films in a window for the children to observe. Talk about what can be seen in the X-rays and how doctors and dentists use them to help treat their patients. If any of the children have ever had an X-ray taken, encourage them to tell about it.

More Ideas for Fun With X

- Form X's with Popsicle sticks or flat toothpicks.
- Draw X's on a sidewalk with colored chalk.
- Search for treasure (small prizes) hidden inside containers that have been marked with X's.
- Form X's with fingers, arms and legs.
- Line up different sizes of posterboard X's from smallest to largest.
- Hop along a path of masking tape X's attached to the floor.
- Play Tic-Tac-Toe.

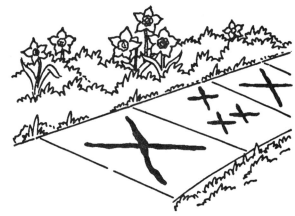

X's Mean Kisses
Sung to: "Skip to My Lou"

X's mean kisses I like a lot,
X is for X-ray and "X marks the spot."
X is for xylophone I like to play,
X is quite extra-special, I'd say.

Elizabeth McKinnon

X Snacks

Set out such foods as stick pretzels, cheese strips, cooked flat noodles or thin flat carrot sticks. Let the children arrange the foods on paper plates in X shapes before eating them. Or use the recipe that follows to make pretzel X's.

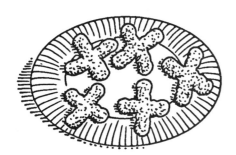

Pretzel X's — Dissolve 1 package yeast in 1 ½ cups warm water and add ½ teaspoon sugar. Add 4 ½ cups flour and knead the dough for 6 minutes. Let the dough rise, covered, in a greased bowl until double in size. Divide the dough into pieces and let the children roll them into sticks. Show the children how to arrange the dough sticks in X shapes. Whisk together 2 tablespoons water and 1 egg yolk and brush the mixture on the pretzel X's. Sprinkle coarse salt or sesame seeds on top. Help the children lay their pretzels on a cookie sheet. Bake at 450 degrees for 12 minutes.

Children's Books:
- *Bodies*, Barbara Brenner, (Dutton).
- *Bugs*, Nancy Parker, (Morrow).
- *Earthhounds as Explained by Professor Xargle*, Jeanne Willis, (Dutton).
- *The Icky Bug Alphabet Book*, Jerry Pallotta, (Charlesbridge).

The Letter X

X-Bug, X-Bug
Sung to: "Jingle Bells"

Late one night, I saw a light
Flying round my head.
It was a teeny tiny bug,
It landed on my bed.
There was an *X* on its back
That glowed when it flew.
I had to name it "X-Bug,"
Wouldn't you too?

X-Bug, X-Bug,
Flying through the air.
X-Bug, X-Bug,
Landing everywhere.
Flying up, flying down,
Your back all aglow.
X's all around my room,
Everywhere you go!

Explain to the children that an X-Bug is an imaginary insect. If desired, repeat the song and let the children draw white *X*'s on black construction paper to show what the X-Bug would look like in a dark room.

Jean Warren

X-Ray Technician Song
Sung to: "Hokey-Pokey"

I put the film in,
I take the film out,
I put the film in
And I turn you all about.
I am a technician
And I take the X-rays out.
That's what it's all about.

I take an X-ray one,
I take an X-ray two,
I take an X-ray three
To show what's inside you.
I am a technician
And I take the X-rays out.
That's what it's all about.

Jean Warren

Contributors:

Betty Ruth Baker, Waco, TX

Alphabet Patterns

Use the patterns on the following pages to make stick puppets, learning games, alphabet books and other teaching aids.

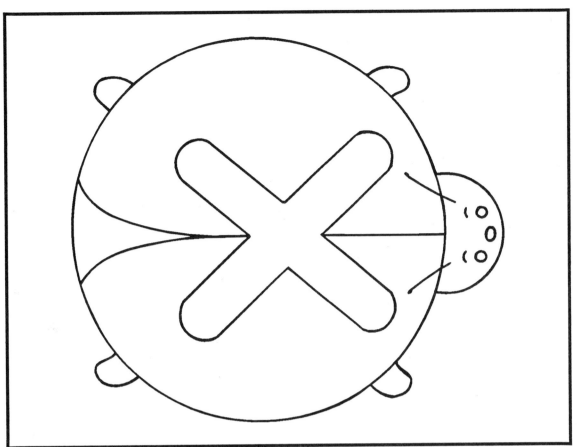

X-bug

X-ray technician

Xx

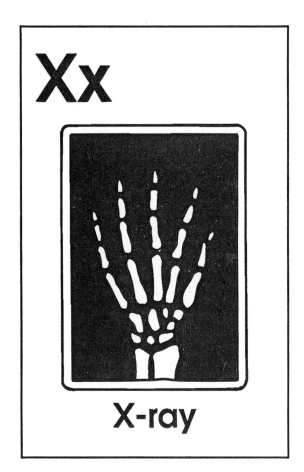

X-ray

Xx

xylophone

The Letter Y

Display/Play Box for Y

Decorate a box with the letter Y to use throughout your Y unit. Inside the box place items (or pictures of items) whose names begin with Y. Below are some suggestions.

- yacht
- yak
- yam
- yardstick
- yarn
- yogurt container
- yo-yo

Yarn Y's

Cut large letter Y shapes out of heavy paper. Set out yarn pieces and shallow containers of glue. Let the children dip the yarn pieces into the glue and then arrange them in designs on their letter shapes.

Young Yolanda

Bring in a yo-yo and demonstrate
how to use it. Then read the poem
below, encouraging the children to
join in on the repeated verses. As
they do so, have them move one
arm up and down like a yo-yo.

Young Yolanda rides a yak,
Sitting proudly on its back.

High, low — High, low.
That's the way the yo-yo goes.

Young Yolanda sails a yacht,
Especially when it's very hot.

High, low — High, low.
That's the way the yo-yo goes.

Young Yolanda does her yoga
In a sunny yellow toga.

High, low — High, low.
That's the way the yo-yo goes.

Young Yolanda just loves yams,
Served up nicely with canned hams.

High, low — High, low.
That's the way the yo-yo goes.

Yolanda yodels in her yard.
That Yolanda's such a card!

High, low — High, low.
That's the way the yo-yo goes.

Yolanda says that yogurt's yummy,
Good and healthy in your tummy.

High, low — High, low.
That's the way the yo-yo goes.

Susan M. Paprocki

The Letter Y

Yellow Collages

Give each child a piece of yellow construction paper or posterboard. Set out glue and yellow collage materials such as scraps of paper and fabric, beads, buttons, yarn and ribbon. Let the children glue the materials on their papers to create yellow collages.

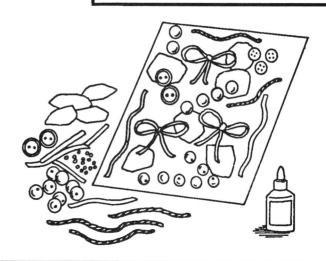

A Yard of Yellow Yarn

Show the children a yardstick and explain how it is used. Stand the yardstick next to one child at a time to see who is tallest. Then let the children help unwind and cut off a yard of yellow yarn. Have them use their yard of yarn to "measure" different objects in the room. Or let them try arranging the yarn on the floor in different shapes.

Y's in Yogurt Cups

Cut small squares out of index cards. Print upper-case Y's on half of the cards and print lower-case Y's on the other half. Set out two empty yogurt cups. Attach one of the upper-case Y squares to one of the cups and one of the lower-case Y squares to the other. Let the children take turns sorting the rest of the squares into the appropriate cups.

Growing a Yam Plant

Use a permanent felt-tip marker to print the letter Y on the side of a large glass jar. Pass around a yam for the children to hold and examine. Then stick several toothpicks into the sides of the yam around the middle. Balance the toothpicks on the rim of the jar and let the children help fill the jar with water. Place the jar in a sunny spot. Each day, have the children check the yam for signs of root and leaf growth. Let them add more water to the jar when necessary. As the yam plant grows, use it to reinforce recognition of the letter Y.

Yes for Y

Print Y's on five or six index cards and print other letters on several more cards. Sit in front of the children and hold up the cards one at a time. Whenever the children see the letter Y, have them say "Yes."

Variation: Have the children say "Yipee!" instead of "Yes."

Yellow Y's

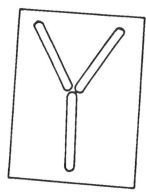

Give each of the children three Popsicle sticks. Let them color their sticks with yellow crayons or felt-tip markers. Hand out sheets of construction paper. Help the children arrange their sticks on their papers in Y shapes. Then let them glue their sticks in place.

The Letter Y

Yodeling Fun

If possible, play musical recordings of yodeling for the children to listen to. (Check your local library for recordings of Swiss or Austrian songs.) Then teach the children how to sing this simple yodel: "Yo-dah-lay-hee-hoo." Ask them to imagine that they are deep in the mountains. Each time they yodel, pretend that you are the echo and answer back.

More Ideas for Fun With Y

- Crack open an egg and observe the yellow yolk.
- Learn what year it is.
- Form Y's on the floor with bodies.
- Learn about the meaning of "Mr. Yuk."
- Do some yoga stretches.
- Have a yawning contest just before naptime.
- Go out in the yard and yell "Yeah!" or "Yahoo!"
- Talk about who is young and who is not young.

Let's Give a Yell for Y

Sung to: "The Farmer in the Dell"

Let's give a yell for Y
Let's give a yell for Y.
Y is for you and for yellow too.
Let's give a yell for Y.

Repeat, substituting other words that begin with Y for the word "yellow."

Elizabeth McKinnon

Yummy Yogurt Snack

At snacktime place such fruits as strawberries, peaches and blueberries in separate bowls. Let the children take turns mashing the fruits with forks. Give each child some plain yogurt in a small bowl. Then let the children spoon the fruits of their choice on top of their yogurt.

Hint: If desired, perk up the taste of the plain yogurt by stirring in a small amount of unsweetened frozen apple juice concentrate.

Children's Books:

- *The Cinnamon Hen's Autumn Day*, Sandra Dutton,(Atheneum).
- *Lucky Yak*, Annetta Lawson, (Houghton Mifflin).
- *Yeh-Shen*, Ed Young, (Putnam).
- *Yuck!*, James Stevenson, (Morrow).

The Letter Y

Yak Song
Sung to: "Three Blind Mice"

Yak, yak, yak; yak, yak, yak,
Has broad shoulders, has a broad back.
He's big and strong and knows the way,
He works hard almost every day,
He doesn't get much time for play.
Yak, yak, yak.

Jean Warren

I Am a Yard Worker
Sung to: "The Mulberry Bush"

Watch me go round the yard today,
Yard today, yard today.
Watch me go round the yard today,
I am a yard worker.

Watch me go round the yard today,
Yard today, yard today.
Watch me go round the yard today,
Mowing all the grass.

Watch me go round the yard today,
Yard today, yard today.
Watch me go round the yard today,
Raking all the leaves.

Additional verses: "Watch me go round the
yard today pruning all the trees; Watch me
go round the yard today planting all the
flowers, etc."

Jean Warren

Contributors:
Betty Ruth Baker, Waco, TX

Alphabet Patterns
Use the patterns on the following
pages to make stick puppets, learning games, alphabet books and
other teaching aids.

yak

yard worker

Yy

yacht

Yy

yak

Yy

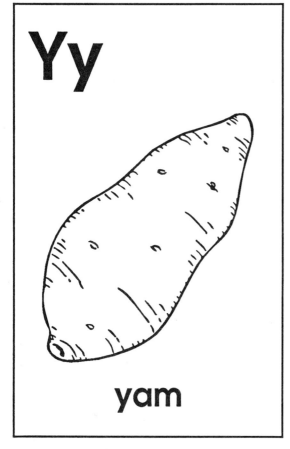

yam

Yy

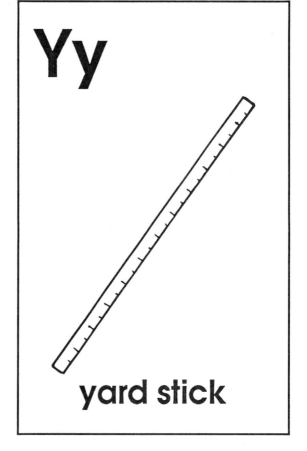

yard stick

Yy

yarn

Yy

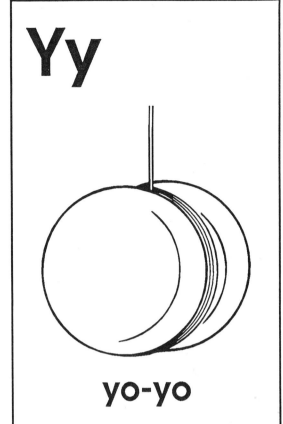

yo-yo

Yy

yogurt

The Letter Z

Display/Play Box for Z

Decorate a box with the letter Z to use throughout your Z unit. Inside the box place items (or pictures of items) whose names begin with Z. Below are some suggestions.

- zebra
- zero
- zinnia
- ZIP code
- zipper
- zither
- zoo
- zucchini
- zwieback

Zipper Z's

Cut large letter Z shapes out of heavy paper. Have on hand a collection of zippers (ask parents or a local tailor to donate broken or unwanted zippers). Give several zippers to each child. Then let the children glue their zippers on their Z shapes.

Variation: Give the children self-stick reinforcement circles (available at stationery stores). Let the children attach the circles to their Z shapes to represent zeros.

Zebra Masks

Give each child a paper plate with eye and nose holes cut out of the center. Have the children paint vertical black stripes on their plates. When the paint has dried, let the children glue precut black ear shapes to the unpainted sides of their plates. Attach yarn ties to the sides of the masks. Or glue tongue depressors to the bottoms of the masks for handles. Let the children use their zebra masks for dramatic play.

Zipper Rubbings

Collect a variety of zippers. Attach them to posterboard squares, if desired. Let the children place sheets of white paper on top of the zippers and rub over them with crayons. Encourage them to fill their papers with different colored zipper rubbings.

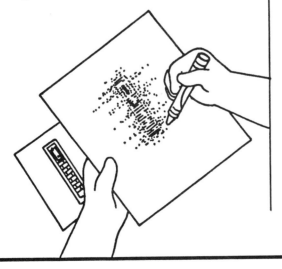

Z Zone Game

Draw a large rectangle on a piece of butcher paper taped to the floor and print "Z Zone" in the center. Talk with the children about different kinds of zones such as school zones, hospital zones and loading zones. Set out your Z Display/Play Box (see page 252). Let the children take turns removing items from the box, naming them and then placing them in the Z zone.

The Letter Z

Z Zigzags

Draw long vertical zigzags down a piece of butcher paper taped to the floor. Let the children use crayons or felt-tip markers to trace over the Z zigzags.

Extension: Use masking tape to create large zigzags on the floor. Let the children walk, crawl, tiptoe and hop along the Z zigzags.

Z Animals in the Zoo

Draw a simple zoo scene on a piece of butcher paper. Print "Z is for Zoo" at the top and hang the paper on a wall at the children's eye level. Cut out construction paper shapes of zoo animals. Print Z's on most of the shapes and print other letters on the rest. Spread out the animal shapes on a table. Let the children take turns selecting animal shapes that are marked with Z's and gluing them on the butcher paper zoo scene.

Zipping Zippers

Set out items that have zippers, such as coats, jackets, handbags and sleeping bags. Let the children have fun zipping and unzipping the zippers. Talk about why some clothes have zippers while others have fasteners like buttons or snaps. Ask the children to tell whether it's easier for them to zip or to button a garment.

Extension: Staple zippers to a cork board for the children to zip and unzip.

Five Little Zinnias

Make five zinnia shapes out of felt and print Z's in the centers. Place the shapes on a flannelboard. Let the children take turns "picking" the zinnias as you read the poem below.

Five little zinnias,
Growing outside my door.
I picked one for Grandma,
Now there are four.

Four little zinnias,
The prettiest I've seen.
I picked one for Grandpa,
Now there are three.

Three little zinnias,
Just a lovely few.
I picked one for Mommy,
Now there are two.

Two little zinnias,
Reaching for the sun.
I picked one for Daddy,
Now there is one.

One little zinnia.
A colorful little hero.
I picked it just for you.
Now there are zero.

Susan M. Paprocki

Extension: Follow up with other counting games that involve the concept of zero.

Zany Z's
Sung to: "London Bridge"

Zany Z's are zipping by,
Zipping by, zipping by.
Zany Z's are zipping by.
Zip! Zap! Zoom!

Zany zebras are zipping by,
Zipping by, zipping by.
Zany zebras are zipping by.
Zip! Zap! Zoom!

Continue with similar verses, substituting other words that begin with Z for the word "zebras."

Rita Galloway

Zither Fun

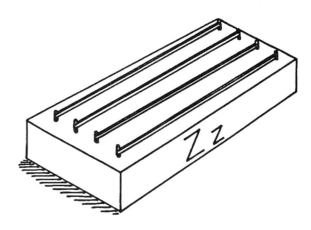

Make a "zither" for the children to play with during your Z unit. Pound nails at opposite ends of a sturdy board and stretch rubber bands from nail to nail as shown in the illustration. Print the letter Z on the side of your zither. Let the children take turns plucking the rubber-band strings as you sing favorite songs.

More Ideas for Fun With Z

- Zoom around like cars, jets or rockets.
- Paint while listening to the song "Zip-A-Dee-Doo-Dah."
- Form Z's on the floor with bodies.
- Listen to recordings of zither music.

- Plant zinnia seeds
- Look for zeros in addresses, license plates, etc.
- Use straws, Popsicle sticks or toothpicks to form Z's

Z Snacks

Let the children spread cream cheese on pieces of zwieback and place zucchini slices on top of the cheese. Or use the recipe below to make zucchini bread.

Zucchini Bread — Heat $\frac{1}{2}$ cup raisins in $\frac{1}{4}$ cup unsweetened frozen apple juice concentrate for about 3 minutes or until the raisins are soft. Puree the mixture in a blender. Add 1 egg, $\frac{1}{4}$ cup vegetable oil, 1 sliced banana and 1 teaspoon vanilla and blend well. In a large bowl mix together 1 cup whole-wheat flour, $\frac{1}{2}$ cup white flour, $\frac{1}{2}$ teaspoon baking powder, $\frac{1}{2}$ teaspoon baking soda and $\frac{1}{4}$ teaspoon salt. Add the ingredients from the blender to the dry ingredients and stir in 1 cup shredded zucchini. Pour the mixture into a greased and floured bread pan and bake at 350 degrees for 50 to 60 minutes.

Children's Books:

- *Children's Zoo*, Tana Hoban, (Macmillan).
- *Sam Who Never Forgets*, Eve Rice, (Morrow).
- *Z Was Zapped*, Chris Van Allsburg, (Houghton Mifflin).
- *Zella, Zack, and Zodiac*, Bill Peet, (Houghton Mifflin).
- *Zug the Bug*, Colin Hawkins, (Putnam).

The Letter Z

I'm a Little Zebra
Sung to: "I'm a Little Teapot"

I'm a little zebra,
White and black,
With a bushy mane
Running down my back.
I like to gallop
And run and play
Out on the African plains
All day.

Jean Warren

Zoo Keeper Song
Sung to: "Down by the Station"

Down at the zoo
Early in the morning, You can see
the animals
Standing in a row.
You can see me feeding
One and then the other.
I am the zoo keeper,
Watch me go!

Down at the zoo
Early in the morning,
You can see the animals
Standing in a row.
You can see me cleaning
One and then the other.
I am the zoo keeper,
Watch me go!

Jean Warren

Contributors:

Betty Ruth Baker, Waco, TX
Jan Bodenstedt, Jackson, MI
Rita Galloway, Harlingen, TX
Susan Peters, Upland, CA

Alphabet Patterns

Use the patterns on the following pages to make stick puppets, learning games, alphabet books and other teaching aids.

zebra

zoo keeper

Zz

zebra

Zz

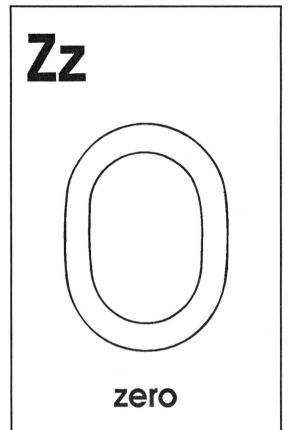

zero

Zz

zinnia

Zz

zip code

Zz

zipper

Zz

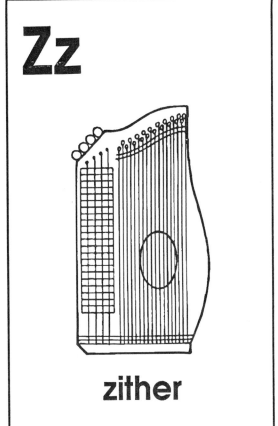

zither

Zz

zoo

Zz

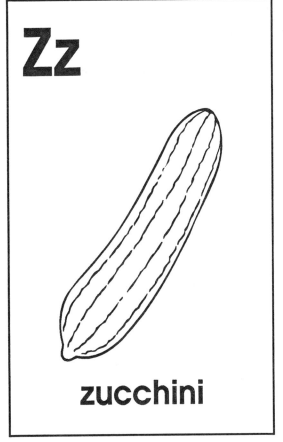

zucchini

Alphabet Review

Alphabet Bulletin Board

Print the letters of the alphabet in the corners of large posterboard squares. As you work with each letter, have the children bring in small items (or pictures of items) whose names begin with that letter. Let the children make a group collage by gluing or taping their items to the posterboard square. Then hang the square as part of a year-long alphabet bulletin board display.

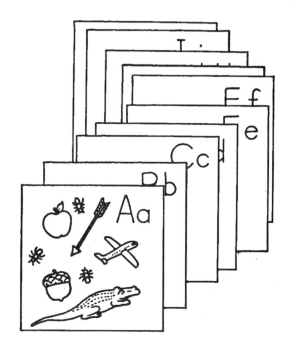

Masking Tape Letters

Use masking tape to form letters on sheets of white construction paper. Let the children marble paint over their letters. When the paint has dried, have the children peel off the masking tape to reveal the unpainted letter shapes.

Variation: Have the children use brushes or sponges to paint over their masking tape letters.

Alphabet Cookie Cutter Prints

Set out alphabet cookie cutters. Place thin flat sponges in shallow containers and pour on small amounts of tempera paint. Let the children make letter prints by pressing the cookie cutters on the sponges and then on sheets of construction paper.

Initials Art

Cut the first letter of each child's name out of construction paper. Let the children decorate their special letters by gluing on sequins or glitter. When the glue has dried, attach each child's letter to a sheet of construction paper and print out the remaining letters of his or her name with a felt-tip marker. Display the papers on a wall or a bulletin board.

Alphabet Review

Letter Rubbings

Cut a set of alphabet letters out of sandpaper and glue them on posterboard squares. Let the children choose the letters they want and arrange them on a tabletop. Have them place pieces of lightweight paper over the letters and rub across them with crayons. Or give one child at a time the letters that appear in his or her first name. Help the child spell out his or her name with the letters and make rubbings of them. Then mount the letter rubbings on heavy colored paper and display them around the room.

Variation: Tape posterboard letter shapes to a tabletop. Have the children place sheets of newsprint on top of the letters and rub across them with crayons.

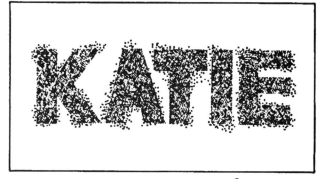

Sponge Letter Prints

Cut different letter shapes out of thin flat sponges (or use sponge letters purchased from a craft store). Set out large sheets of construction paper and pour tempera paint into shallow containers. Let the children dip the sponge letters into the paint and press them on their papers to make prints.

Variation: Add soap powder to the paint and let the children sponge print letters on windows or glass doors.

Playdough Letters

Set out balls of playdough and let the children pat or roll them out flat. Then let them use alphabet cookie cutters to cut letters out of the playdough. Use this activity to review specific letters. Or have the children cut out their initials or the letters that spell their names.

Alphabet Accordion Book

Fold thirteen large index cards in half. Then unfold the cards and tape them together end to end. (Tape both sides of the cards for a more durable book.) Label the sections of the cards from A to Z. On each section glue a small picture of something whose name begins with the letter that is printed on it. Fold the cards together accordion style. Use the book for "reading" at circle time or stand it on a low shelf or table for the children to look at.

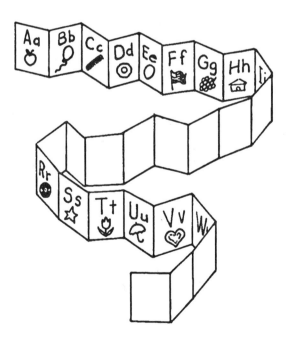

Alphabet Review

Letter Notebook

Make a notebook by punching holes in the tops of 27 index cards and inserting small metal rings. Use felt-tip markers to print "Letter Notebook" on the first card. Then starting with *A*, print an upper- and lower-case letter of the alphabet on each of the remaining cards. Let the children have fun turning the pages of the notebook, naming the letters and tracing over them with their fingers.

Variation: Instead of making the notebook from individual cards, purchase a spiral-bound set of index cards from a stationery store.

ABC Scrapbook

Use a scrapbook to create your own ABC picture book. Cut alphabet letters out of sandpaper or flocked wallpaper and glue one letter on each page. Then glue on a picture of something whose name begins with that letter. (Use pictures cut from magazines or from coloring books.) Let the children take turns looking through the book, touching the textured letters and naming the pictures.

Alphabet Take-Home Items

To reinforce letter recognition, provide the children with related alphabet items that they can take home. For example, print C's on paper cookie shapes to reinforce the letter C. Place the cookies in a cookie jar and let each child reach in and take one. For the letter E, let the children choose paper egg shapes that have been marked with E's and placed in an egg basket. And for the letter M, use a monkey puppet to hand out play money that has been labeled with M's.

Alphabet Puppets

Use Popsicle sticks, magazine pictures and pasta alphabet letters to create alphabet puppets. To make each puppet, glue a pasta letter on the center part of a Popsicle stick. At the top of the stick, glue a picture of something whose name begins with that letter. Make several puppets for each letter or make a set for the entire alphabet. When the glue has dried, let the children use the puppets while telling stories or singing songs.

Alphabet Review

Alphabet Roll

Collect or make alphabet cards that contain letters and pictures for several letters you wish to review. Have the children sit on the floor in a semicircle. Start the game by rolling a ball to one of the children. Hold up an alphabet card and have the child name the letter and the picture. Then have the child roll the ball back to you. Continue in the same manner until every child has had a turn.

Alpha-Bag

Make or purchase a brightly colored drawstring bag. Make several alphabet cards each for three or more letters and place them around the room. Give the bag to a child and ask him or her to go on a *C* Hunt, a *G* Hunt, etc. Have the child find the appropriate cards, place them in the bag and bring them back to you. Continue until each child has had a turn.

Variation: Print different letters on Post-it brand notes and attach them to objects whose names begin with those letters. Have the children use the alpha-bag to collect all the *B* objects, all the *D* objects, etc.

Letter Hide and Seek

If desired, make a special set of posterboard alphabet letters to use for this game. Each morning, hide six to eight of the letters around the room in places where the children are likely to come across them as they work or play. Whenever a child finds a letter, have the child bring it to you and tell you its name. If any letters are still hidden at the end of the day, let the children search for them as a group.

Touch and Match Letters

Choose several letters you wish to review. For each letter cut out two small posterboard squares. Use a brush dipped in glue to print the letter on the two cards. Then sprinkle on sand. When the glue has dried, set out the cards. Let the children trace over the textured letters with their fingers to find the matching pairs.

Variation: Form each pair of matching letters by gluing on a different kind of material such as yarn, ribbon, rice, glitter, dried beans or buttons.

Extension: Place the textured letter cards in a paper bag. Let the children take turns reaching into the bag and identifying the letters by touch.

Alphabet Review

Alphabet Mail Game

Make mailboxes by covering the lids of three shoeboxes with construction paper and cutting a slit in the top of each lid. Put the lids on the boxes. Print different upper-case letters on three index cards and tape them to the backs of the mailboxes so that they stand above the lids. For each mailbox print a matching upper- or lower-case letter on the fronts of five sealed envelopes. Then mix up the envelopes and let the children take turns "mailing" them through the slots in the mailboxes. Each day, change the cards on the mailboxes and make new envelopes to review different letters.

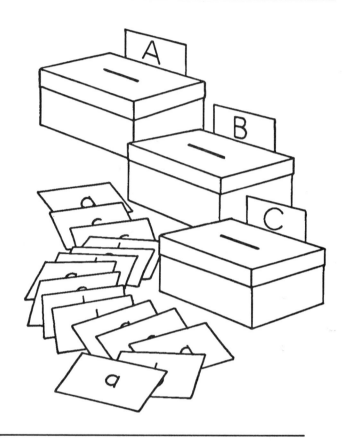

Alphabet Block Match

Print letters or simple words on index cards. Place the cards and a set of alphabet blocks on a table. Let the children select cards and find alphabet blocks that match the letters on the cards.

Variation: Print the children's names on large index cards. Let the children match the alphabet blocks to the letters in their names.

Alphabet Clothesline

Tie a clothesline between two chairs and clip on 26 clothespins. Cut 26 small sock shapes out of construction paper. Label the socks from A to Z and place them in a basket. Let the children take turns choosing a sock shape, naming the letter on it and clipping it to the clothesline. Continue until each child has had a turn or until all the socks have been hung on the line.

Variation: Collect old unmatched socks to use for this game. Label the socks with embroidered or ironed-on letters.

Letter Lotto

Make a gameboard by dividing a 9-inch square of posterboard into nine squares. Print a different upper-case letter in each square. Cut nine 3-inch game cards out of posterboard and print matching upper- or lower-case letters on them. Tape a large envelope to the back of the gameboard to hold the game cards. To play, have the children name the letters on the game cards and then place them on top of the matching letters on the gameboard.

Alphabet Review

Letter Windows

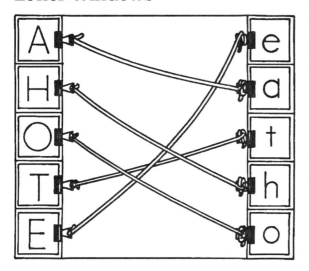

Tape a row of clear plastic photo holders down each side of a large sheet of posterboard. Attach a metal paper fastener next to each photo holder, toward the center of the board. Cut index cards to fit inside the photo holders. Print upper-case letters on one set of cards and insert them in the photo holders in the left-hand row. Make a matching set of upper- or lower-case letter cards and insert them in the photo holders in the right-hand row in a different order. Tie short pieces of yarn to the paper fasteners on the left. Then let the children match the cards by winding the loose ends of the yarn pieces around the appropriate paper fasteners on the right. Change the cards in the photo holders each day to review different alphabet letters.

Alpha-Match Puzzles

Use 8- by 10-inch posterboard rectangles to make puzzles for the letters of the alphabet. To make each puzzle, cut a rectangle into three puzzle pieces. Use a felt-tip marker to print an upper-case letter on the left-hand piece and a matching lower-case letter on the right-hand piece. On the middle piece draw a picture of something whose name begins with the printed letter. Set out the pieces of several puzzles at a time and let the children have fun putting them together.